OVER THE TOP

A Cookbook by Debra Sampson

© 2005 Debra Sampson
All Rights Reserved.

No part of this book may be reproduced, stored in a retrieval system, or transmitted by any means without the written permission of the author.

First published by AuthorHouse 11/15/04

ISBN: 1-4184-9741-X (sc)

Library of Congress Control Number: 2004099128

Printed in the United States of America
Bloomington, Indiana

This book is printed on acid-free paper.

Cover design by Jason Parker

1663 LIBERTY DRIVE
BLOOMINGTON, INDIANA 47403
(800) 839-8640
www.authorhouse.com

To Dotty

who ignited the spark,

gave me my first Julia Child cookbook

and a subscription to Gourmet,

which fuels the fire to this day.

In memory of

Toby Dachs, the best-ever.

Acknowledgements

Jim, Julie, and Anne (Sam - sous extraordinaire) are my dearest friends, my most valued consultants, and an endless source of empathy, light-hearted ribbing, encouragement, and laughter. With John as sommelier, Rick on the grill at the Cape, and Birgit at the cutting board, we dine in culinary bliss. Sara, Emily, and Victoria infuse my life with more comedy and love than any aunt could wish for. My entire family is my greatest asset.

Dine by Design owes its reputation primarily to the competence, friendliness, and professionalism of its incredible staff. They never have a harsh word, even when I really, really deserve it. How can work be so much fun?

And then there's Joe. He dissolves my fears, nourishes my creativity, coaches me through bad days, and for 21 years has tearfully eaten my grilled salmon and jalapeno chowder. He is the sweetest, funniest, most irreverent man I know. Without him hot pepper pizza would taste bland, and Heineken would be flat.

About the Author

Debra Sampson was raised in Massachusetts and worked in the restaurant business after college. She has owned and operated her catering company, Dine by Design, since 1983.

Table of Contents

Introduction and Words to the Party-wise ix
Cooking Notes and Purveyors xi
Garni – every platter must have one xii

Pancakes and Fritters, Cornmeal and Biscuits 1

- Sweet Potato and Jalapeno Fritters with Cilantro Cream and Shrimp 3
- Habanero Corncakes with Ham, Melted Swiss, and Grapefruit Cream 4
- Shepherd's Pie on Creamed Corncakes with Mashed Potatoes 7
- Vidalia Onion Fritters with Smoked Salmon and Dill 9
- Leek Polenta with Mango Mojo 11
- Creamed Salmon with Chives on Mini-Biscuit Bites 13
- Saffron Scallops with Cilantro Shallot Cream on Buttermilk Cornbread 15
- Red Onion Arepas with Mozzarella and Tomato 16

Meat and Fish Nuggets Toothpick Morsels 18

- Ground Veal and Shallots in a Balsamic Vinegar Sauce 19
- Lamb, Garlic, and Basil Nuggets in a Curried Red Pepper Pureé 21
- Grilled Salmon Cakes with Pineapple Salsa 22
- Turkey Parmesan with Melted Mozzarella in a Spicy Marinara Sauce 24
- African Lamb Babotie with Nutmeg Custard 27
- Spicy Pork and Garlic Sausage in a Saffron Lime Sauce 28
- Crab Cakes with Mustard Sauce 30
- Beef Tenderloin with Béarnaise Sauce 31
- Ginger, Jalapeno, and Yogurt Tandoori Chicken with a Thai Peanut Dip 32
- Tupelo Honey Scallops in a Chipotle Lime Hollandaise 33
- Jamaican Jerk Pork in a Saffron Sauce with Pink Peppercorn Olives 34

Quesadillas and Tortillas 35

- Roquefort, Merlot Apple, and Walnut Quesadillas with Cardamom Applesauce 37
- Seared Tuna Soft Tacos with Jalapenos 38
- Grilled Chicken and Chipotle Pepper Quesadillas 39
- Shrimp, Feta, and Arugula Quesadillas with Lime 40
- Mushroom Quesadillas with Marsala and Basil 41
- Black Bean Nachos with Avocado, Cheddar, and Sour Cream 43
- Bourbon BBQ Beef and Sage Quesadillas 44
- Cactus Quesadillas with Cilantro 45

Crostini and Frittata 46

- Gruyere Scallop Crostini with Dill 48
- Shrimp, Jalapeno, and Goat Cheese Crostini 49
- Pistachio, Cilantro, and Jalapeno Bruschetta with Marinated Tomatoes 50
- Eggplant and Oregano or Shiitake Mushrooms with St. André Cheese Crostini 51
- Poached Pear, Brie, and Pommery Crostini 54
- Cuttlefish Ink Frittata with Leeks and Smoked Salmon 56
- Artichoke, Habanero, and Basil Crostini 57
- Olive, Arugula, and Habanero Frittata 58

Crispy Critters 59

- Lamb Racks in a Rosemary Crust with Dijon 60
- Spiced Beef Wellingtons 62
- Peking Duck with Scallions in Couscous Cups 63
- Yukon Gold Ginger Cakes with Sour Cream and Caviar or Hoisin Sauce 64
- Crispy Buttermilk Pecan Chicken with a Curried Horseradish Dip 65
- Sherried Lobster Newburg with Leeks in Vol-au-Vent Shells 67
- Spicy Stuffed Mushrooms with Tomatillos 68
- Spanish Clams Casino in Black Rye Cups 69
- Moroccan Swordfish 71
- Tonkatsu with a Tamarind Dip 74

Cold Canapés 75

- Lemon, Garlic, and Dill Shrimp Cocktail with a Spicy Cocktail Sauce 76
- Sherried Shallot Liver Pureé on Red Apples 78
- Scallop Citrus Ceviche in Belgian Endive 79
- Spicy Steak Tartare 82
- Smoked Salmon Mousse on Cukes with Horseradish Cream 83
- Lemon Coconut Rice Slices with Tuna Tartare 86
- Rolled Saffron Crepes with Jalapenos 87
- Prosciutto and Shaved Parmesan with Tomato and Basil Leaf 89

Finger Sandwiches 90

- Spicy Goat Cheese and Prosciutto Croque Monsieurs 92
- Lobster Knuckles with Lime and Shallots in Hot Dog Rolls 93
- Crab and Shrimp Salad with Lemon, Ranch Dressing 93
- Roasted Tenderloin with Béarnaise Mayo on Sourdough 94
- Cranberry Sauce 94
- Roast Turkey and Lemon Thyme Stuffing with Cranberry Sauce 95
- Grilled Salmon Salad Pitas with Capers and Peppercorn Pyrennes Cheese 96

Hummus, Spinach, and Roasted Pepper Pitas 97

Sweets 98

    Chocolate Chip and Oatmeal Cookies with Almonds and Coconut 100
    Viennese Lemon Cakes 100
    White Chocolate Bark with Cranberries and Pistachios 101
    Tuaca-Laced Gingerbread with Lemon Cream 101
    Walnut Carrot Cake with Cream Cheese Frosting 104
    Baby Key Lime Pies with a Chocolate Cardamom Crust 104
    Soft Chocolate Espresso Clouds 105
    Pecan Brownies 105

List of Pictures

#1 - Sweet Potato Fritters with Shrimp
#2 - Habanero Corncakes with Ham and Swiss
#3 - Shepherd's Pie
#4 - Leek Polenta with Shiitake Mushrooms
#5 - Leek Polenta with Mango Mojo
#6 - Grilled Tuna with Shallot Cream on Cornbread
#7 - Red Onion Arepas with Mozzarella and Tomato
#8 - Lamb and Basil Nuggets in a Red Pepper Pureé
#9 - Grilled Salmon Cakes with Pineapple Salsa on Asian Seaweed
#10 - African Lamb Babotie with Nutmeg Custard
#11 - Spicy Pork Sausage in a Saffron Lime Sauce
#12 - Roquefort, Walnut, and Apple Quesadillas
#13 - Black Bean Nachos
#14 - Gruyere Scallop Crostini
#15 - Shiitake Mushroom Crostini with Portabellas
#16 - Poached Pear and Brie Crostini
#17 - Cuttlefish Ink Frittata with Smoked Salmon
#18 - Spiced Beef Wellingtons on Red Bean Threads
#19 - Crispy Buttermilk Chicken with a Thai Peanut Dip
#20 - Spanish Clams Casino
#21 - Tonkatsu with a Tamarind Dip and Yukon Gold Ginger Cakes
#22 - Moroccan Swordfish with a Saffron Lime Dip
#23 - Sherried Liver Pureé on Red Apples
#24 - Scallop Ceviche in Belgian Endive
#25 - Spicy Steak Tartare
#26 - Smoked Salmon Mousse on Cukes
#27 - Lemon Coconut Rice Slices with Cilantro and Lobster Knuckles
#28 - Rolled Saffron Crepes
#29 - Croque Monsieurs with Prosciutto and Parmesan Canapés
#30 - Amazing Chocolate Chip Cookies
#31 - Bark, Brownies, Gingerbread, and Key Lime Pies
#32 - Walnut Carrot Cake and Viennese Lemon Cakes

Introduction

When was the last time you left a cocktail party saying "that was the best sugar snap pea I've ever had!?" Although simple food does have its place, and nothing satisfies me quite like a warm, yeasty mouthful of unadorned bread, it won't make your party memorable. But...brush that bread with butter...crisp the edges to please the eye...spread it with a creamy St. André cheese awakened with vidalias and lemon...top that with musky shiitakes scented with Marsala and basil...sprinkle it with Asiago and freshly cracked pepper, and send your taste buds on the ride of their little pink lives. You choose...smooth, spicy, citrusy, crispy crostini or pea? Bright simple garnishes and old-fashioned veggie canapés do provide crunchy and colorful accompaniments to cocktail presentations, but they'll never thrill your guests. This mushroom crostini is one of many recipes for finger food and light dining which attempts to please all your senses on every possible culinary level. Whichever ones the spices fail to stimulate, the ensuing conversations about their colorful presentations will.

Don't be put off by the number of ingredients in these recipes. Great food has depth and dimension. It unfolds on the palate with distinctive layers of flavor that emerge from first bite (often citrus) to the savoring process (sometimes herbal) to the lingering finish (usually spicy). Each ingredient individually participates in and contributes to this process. Omitting one spice will result in a less complex creation, not necessarily an unsuccessful one. Their preparation and assembly require neither great cooking expertise, nor esoteric foodstuffs, nor Stewartesque familiarity with the pastry bag. Your reward will be the appreciative moans of your guests and leftovers very happily frozen.

So choreograph that cocktail party fare, cook everything in advance, gather your hungriest friends, then relax. This food alone has the personality to entertain a crowd...it's over the top!

Words to the Party-wise

Because my catering career has honed my cooking instincts, these recipes aim to please the masses, not the purists. Worcestershire instead of tamarind pulp approaches sacrilege, and just 3 cloves of garlic in a tandoori marinade seem sinfully inadequate, but these recipes will satisfy a broad range of tastes because nothing is extreme and seasonings are fully rounded. Citrus, salt, spice, heat, and sweetness linger throughout, while few flavors overwhelm. I marinate lamb to taste less like mutton...sherry or lemon is added to keep fishiness at bay...salt, sugar, or stock often enhance the sometimes thin or bitter flavor of imperfect vegetables.

Season to taste with a consideration of all guests.

- For a successful party pleasing all palates, temper your garlic addiction and consider whether your friends crave the breathy cloves as much as you. To tame it somewhat, warm it only briefly at a low heat. If it browns, toss it, or it'll ruin everything. I always use a garlic press, making it easily and evenly incorporated into dips if raw or butter to heat. Minced garlic never distributes its flavor so uniformly and subtly. Use similar caution with jalapenos and other killer spices. A choking crowd is not necessarily a lively one. If you want to get fiery, put the heat in

- a sauce on the side offering everyone a choice.
- Don't serve shrimp with tails, pineapple with rind, strawberries with stems, or sugar snaps with strings. What are people supposed to do with the refuse? An exception allows cherries with pits and possibly olives, but leave small trash bowls nearby.
- Toothpicks, yes. Skewers, no...not for finger food. The former are a necessary evil, so have containers right on the platter to collect them...halved limes or other soft fruits to stick used ones in.
- Food Snob Alert! You don't have time to do it all, so pick your short-cuts. I use Minor's chicken, veal, fish, mushroom, and vegetable stock bases for seasoning, often as the only salt addition, and as a liquid stock. I use Hidden Valley Ranch Dressing Mix with Hellman's mayo for many salad dressings. If I can't easily and quickly make something better than store-bought, I buy it. The same goes for Goya adobo seasoning, which is mostly salt, onion, and spices. I never get tired of its flavor on anything grilled. A good store bought hot salsa works well as a dunk for quesadillas when brightened with a squirt of ketchup for necessary thickness and color. Try Mrs. Renfro's hot green salsa.
- Don't mess with fat or salt contents in these recipes for a party. You'll defeat the intention of presenting well-seasoned, luxurious food. Besides, I've already reduced fats to the verge of sacrificing flavor or texture, and you shouldn't need more salt with these stock bases.
- Never broil or roast anything in extra virgin olive oil. It splatters all over your oven. When sautéing, I usually use vegetable oil which withstands long-term high heat the best. A quick sauté calls for a more nutritious light olive oil.
- Sometimes fresh, hot peppers... sometimes in jars? Preserved are more predictable and tender, particularly with habaneros, but always seed them. Fresh habaneros' heat is way over the top to many and hard to measure. Don't use these beautifully colored peppers as a fresh garnish...they'll be trouble if anyone pops one whole. Fresh jalapenos, seeded, are tame. Using them with seeds to yield even heat is tough, but many recipes need their color or crispness. Trust that nothing is killer hot in these recipes but play with it if you're sensitive.
- Crunch is overrated and translates to tough with many hors d'oeuvres where reheating may be necessary. Rock-hard crostini or bruschetta is popular with many, but I don't get it. Tender morsels rule at parties.
- Garnish every platter with fresh fruit or prepped veggies. This provides contrasting color as edible garnish, spares you of making labor-intensive crudité platters, and pleases dieters, picky eaters, and the lactose-intolerant.
- Vegetarians should always be considered. Simply omit the meat or fish topping and substitute a slice of jalapeno on just a few pieces. Try this on fritters, pancakes, cornbread, potato cakes, and rice slices.
- I do not recommend freezing any hors d'oeuvres for a party. They should be chilled as instructed (well-wrapped) and assembled right before the party.

Cooking Notes and Purveyors

t = teaspoon
T = tablespoon
butter = regular, salted butter
eggs = large
shallots, garlic, onion, leeks = large
lemon and lime juices are always fresh-squeezed.
1 lemon zest = the zest only of one lemon (and they're easier to squeeze after zesting)
cream cheese = Philadelphia brand...it's firmer
bread crumbs = Japanese Panko Bread Crumbs...lighter, whiter, and fresher

Many recipes use stock bases. My favorites are Minor's...chicken, veal, fish, mushroom, and vegetable. Because they are a paste, they must be carefully and completely incorporated into the sauce. They often provide the only salt in the recipe, so don't substitute with a low-salt (often vegetarian) alternative. You then must add salt to compensate. A good store 'soup base' is Carmel 'tastes like chicken' or 'mushroom' in the kosher section. They're parve so it's vegetarian as well. It does contain some MSG. Another is Knorr's. Avoid hard cubes, as they're harder to soften and blend.

Microwave instructions are all on high in a big machine. Carefully increase time as needed if your micro is little or old. Be very careful warming egg yolks. Process is to mix in food processor...you may need to do this in batches. Pulse is to use on/off switch to carefully blend in food processor.

All sauces, reductions, and sautés require intermittent stirring. Cook on medium for 5 minutes means to stir every minute or two.

To clarify butter, cook on medium for 15 minutes until clear (swirling the pan helps). The white, creamy milk solids will sink to the bottom of the pan. Save this. The richness of my hollandaise, lime hollandaise, chipotle hollandaise, and béarnaise lies in the use of milk solids remaining from clarified butter in place of salt in the recipe. Usually 2 T milk solids = ¼ t salt. You may need to adjust this or use a bit of both.

All ingredients should be at room temperature for cooking and reheating. If hors d'oeuvres have been frozen, thaw at room temperature for 1-2 hours or overnight in the fridge.

Grate onion on the large side of a box grater or with food processor grater. Use your hand to squeeze out moisture, if required, usually 'til very dry. Try to get vidalias or Texas sweets. Grate cheeses on large side of a box grater or with food processor grater. Parmesan, Asiago, and Romano are exceptions. Use small side of grater. For quesadillas, it's easiest to buy cheeses already grated.

Frozen hors d'oeuvres are only as good as their wrapping. Quesadillas should be layered in wax paper then sealed in a zip baggie. Most others, if assembled, should be wrapped in plastic, layered with wax paper (as snugly as possible) then enclosed in foil. Nothing should be frozen for longer than 2 weeks, though you can get away with a month on some unassembled items such as fritters and quesadillas. For sweets, only the brownies do well in the freezer.

Do not interchange fresh and dried herbs. Follow the recipe.

I use the slightly larger mini-muffin pans with a 2" width at the top.

Local Purveyors

Lobster – James Hook in Boston
Produce – Russo's in Watertown
Seafood – North Coast Seafoods in Boston (mostly wholesale, but they sell to Star Market)
Deli Meats, some specialty seafood, spices, and grocery – Marty's in Newton
Specialty Meats – John Dewar in Newton
Stock Bases – Minor's Mail Order – 800-827-8328
Asian Foods – Jin Mi Oriental Market in Newtonville
Cheeses and Boyajian oils and caviars – Whole Foods Market
Bread – Great Harvest in Newtonville
Party Rentals – Peterson's in Winchester
Flowers – Brattle Square Florist in Cambridge

Garni - every platter must have one

BEAN THREADS: Soak threads in hot water for 15 minutes. Drain and dry. Mix dye in bowl. Toss in threads and let sit. Wrap in paper towel and seal in baggie.
Purple=5 blue+5 red
Pale Blue=1 blue+1 T water
Dark Olive=3 green+1 red+1 blue+1 yellow
Salmon=3 red+2 yellow+1 T water
Deep Crimson=6 red+1 blue
Deep Mustard=4 yellow+1 red+1 green
May do 4 days in advance.
GREEN VEGGIES: Asparagus, sugar snap peas, snow peas, and broccoli should all be cooked to bring out color and to tenderize. I cook them in rolling boiling water 'til barely tender, then plunge them in cold water for one minute. Drain. Re-chill water and immerse again 'til veggies are completely cold. Drain, dry, and wrap in paper towel and seal in baggie. May do 1 day in advance.
ORANGE, YELLOW, AND RED PEPPERS: Cut in long wedges then wrap in paper towel and seal in baggie. May do 2 days in advance.
FRESH CORN: Husk corn and cover with cold water in pan. Cover and cook on high to a rolling boil. Remove cover and let sit 5 minutes. Drain, cool, and chill in baggie overnight. Stand corn on end and beginning at the middle, slice down to the bottom. Do this on all 4 sides. Invert corn and again, cut from the middle down to bottom of ear, repeating on all 4 sides. Wrap carefully

and seal in baggie. May do 2 days in advance.

GRAPE TOMATOES: Wash and return to container, lined with paper towels. OR let sit in a sunny window and sun-ripen 'til shriveled...discard any that go soft. Serve in bowls.

LETTUCES: Cut off core. Wash, shake off water, then wrap in paper towels. Seal in baggie. May do 2 days in advance.

JARLSBERG, CHEDDAR, and COLBY: Cut in triangles, rectangles, or squares. Wrap tightly in plastic and seal in baggie. May do 4 days in advance.

CRANBERRIES: Freeze in the fall for the whole year. Thaw as needed.

STRAWBERRIES: Cut off stems flat and wrap in paper towel. Store in Tupperware. May do 1 day in advance. Pile flat side down on platter.

CANTALOUPE and PINEAPPLE: Remove skin and core, then cup in bite-sized pieces. Wrap in paper towels and seal in baggie. May do 1 day in advance.

PEARS or GREEN APPLES: Slice and seal in baggie with 2 T lemon juice, 1 T water, and 1 T sugar. May do 1 hour in advance.

BLACKBERRIES and RASPBERRIES: Wipe clean. Pile stem side down.

SPICED PECANS: (adapted from *Saveur Magazine*) Bake 6 cups pecans at 350 for 10 minutes. Mix 3 T melted butter, 3 T brown sugar, 1 t cayenne, 2 T fresh rosemary, minced, and 1 t salt. Toss nuts, cool, and seal in zip baggie. Chill.
May do 4 days in advance. Serve in bowls.

USED TOOTHPICK COLLECTORS: halved lemon, lime, orange, pomegranate, grapefruit, blood orange, or tomato

Pancakes and Fritters

Sweet Potato and Jalapeno Fritters with Cilantro Cream and Shrimp

Habanero Corncakes with Ham, Melted Swiss, and Grapefruit Cream

Shepherd's Pie on Creamed Corncakes with Mashed Potatoes

Vidalia Onion Fritters with Smoked Salmon and Dill

Leek Polenta with Mango Mojo

Creamed Salmon with Chives on Mini-Biscuits

Saffron Scallops with Cilantro, Shallot Cream on Buttermilk Cornbread

Red Onion Arepas with Mozzarella and Tomato

Sweet Potato Fritters with Shrimp

Sweet Potato Fritters with Cilantro and Shrimp

makes 60 hors, 75 fritters

1 lb. sweet potato, peeled 1 onion	Coarsely grate sweet potato and onion in processor.
5 eggs 8 oz. hot verde salsa (green) 2 T jalapeno (jar), minced 1 ½ cup flour	Mix eggs, salsa, and jalapenos. Add potato and onion, then flour. Let sit 15 minutes to absorb flour.
1 cup vegetable oil	Heat oil to medium-high. Drop batter in wet forkfuls. Cook for 1-2 minutes each side. Drain on paper towel. Proceed, Refrigerate, or Freeze.
8 oz. cream cheese, soft 2 T lemon juice 1 sweet onion, grated and squeezed dry ¼ t salt ¼ cup cilantro, chopped	Mix cream cheese, lemon, onion pulp, salt, then cilantro. Place in a baggie. Chill to firm.
2 lbs. medium shrimp, cooked, tail off	Cut off a small corner of the baggie. Pipe a teaspoon of cheese on each fritter. Top with a shrimp. Bake at 300 for 4 minutes. (The cheese should warm slightly but not soften too much).

Garni: whole jalapenos, snow peas, or red pepper strips

Habanero Corncakes with Ham, Swiss, and Grapefruit Cream

makes 60 pieces

3 T butter	Melt butter, add brown sugar, then remove from heat.
2 T brown sugar	

1 cup flour
¼ cup cornmeal
½ t baking soda
½ t salt
2 eggs
¼ cup vegetable oil
½ t habanero pepper (jar), seeded and minced
½ cup water

Mix flour, cornmeal, baking soda, and salt. Add eggs, oil, sugar butter, and habanero.

Add enough water to consistency of thick batter.
Heat skillet to medium and butter lightly.

3 T butter for pan

Drop batter by spoonfuls, and cook 1 minute each side.

½ lb. Black Forest Ham, thinly sliced
¼ lb. Jarlsberg, thinly sliced, cut in small triangles

Top each pancake with a folded ham slice, then with a slice of Swiss.
Proceed, Refrigerate, or Freeze.

4 oz. cream cheese, soft
½ t grapefruit zest, minced
1 t grapefruit juice concentrate (frozen)
1 T lemon juice
½ sweet onion, grated and squeezed dry
¼ t paprika
1/8 t salt

Mix cream cheese, grapefruit zest, grapefruit concentrate, lemon, onion, paprika, and salt. Place in a baggie. Chill to firm.

Bake corncakes at 350 for 5 minutes.
Cut off a small corner of the baggie.
Pipe on a dollop of grapefruit cream.

Habanero Corncakes with Ham and Swiss

Shepherd's Pie

Shepherd's Pie on Creamed Corncakes with Mashed Potatoes

makes 40 pieces or serves 4 light dining

1 T olive oil	Heat oil and cook lamb on medium for 10 minutes, breaking it up. Cool.
¾ lb. ground lamb	
1 T butter	Heat butter and cook flour on low for 5 minutes. Cool slightly.
1 T flour	
¼ t thyme, powdered	Add thyme, pepper, stock base, then garlic. Warm on low 1 minute.
1 t black pepper	
1 t veal or chicken stock base	
2 garlic, pressed	
¼ cup port	Add port then cream. Cook 'til smooth. Pour any fat off lamb then add lamb to sauce with scallions. Warm briefly then cool. Add egg yolk, corn, panko, and parsley. Chill.
2 T heavy cream	
6 scallions, minced	
1 egg yolk	
1 cup corn	
2 T panko bread crumbs	
¼ cup fresh parsley, chopped	
2 potatoes, peeled and quartered	Boil potatoes in water for 15 minutes. Drain and mash over low heat. Off heat add butter, onion powder, egg yolk, cream, and salt.
2 T butter, melted	
¼ t onion powder	
1 egg yolk	
¼ cup heavy cream	
¼ t salt	

Note: Have butcher custom grind lamb, completely trimmed of fat. The bulk pre-ground lamb is too fatty.

Creamed Corncakes
makes 40 pieces

4 T butter	Melt butter and cook jalapenos on medium for 5 minutes.
2 jalapenos, minced with seeds	
1 cup flour	Combine flour, cornmeal, baking powder, salt, and sugar.
½ cup yellow cornmeal	
½ t baking powder	
½ t salt	
1 T sugar	
2 eggs	Add eggs, creamed corn, oil, jalapenos, and buttermilk.
1 cup creamed corn	
¼ cup light olive oil	
1/3 cup buttermilk	
4 T butter for pan	Heat skillet to medium and butter lightly. Drop batter by spoonfuls. Cook 1-2 minutes each side.
chives, cut in ½" pieces	Spoon lamb onto corncake and pipe potato on top. Garnish with chives. Proceed, Refrigerate, or Freeze.
	Bake at 350 for 5 minutes.

Garni: fresh corn off the cob
Note: You may want cocktail plates with these.
Options: Make full-sized corncakes for light dining.

Vidalia Onion Fritters with Smoked Salmon and Dill

makes 30 pieces

½ lb. Yukon Gold potatoes, washed
1 vidalia onion

Coarsely grate unpeeled potato and onion in processor.

2 eggs
1 ½ t black pepper
½ t salt
1 cup flour
2 T fresh sage, chopped

Mix eggs, pepper, salt, potato, onion, then flour and sage. Let sit 10 minutes.

½ cup vegetable oil
salt, for sprinkling

Heat oil to medium-high.
Drop batter in wet forkfuls.
Cook for 1-2 minutes each side.
Drain on paper towel. Salt.
Proceed, Refrigerate, or Freeze.

4 oz. cream cheese, soft
1 T lemon juice
½ sweet onion, grated and squeezed dry
1/8 t salt
1 T fresh dill, chopped

Mix cream cheese, lemon, onion pulp, salt, then dill. Place in a baggie. Chill to firm.

Cut off a small corner of the baggie.
Pipe a teaspoon of cheese on each fritter.
Bake at 300 for 4 minutes. (The cheese should warm slightly but not soften too much).
Top with smoked salmon.

½ lb. smoked salmon, cut in ½" strips

Options: Substitute 1 T wasabi mixed in 1 T water for the dill in the cream topping.

Leek Polenta with Shiitake Mushrooms

Leek Polenta with Mango Mojo

makes 50 pieces or serves 8 for light dining

3 T butter
2 leeks, white only, chopped
3 garlic, pressed

Melt 3 T butter and cook leeks on medium for 8 minutes.
Add garlic and heat on low 1 minute.

4 cups chicken stock
(1 t base per 1 cup of water)
4 T butter
1 cup yellow cornmeal
6 oz. goat cheese

Boil liquid stock with butter.
Whisk in cornmeal.
Cook on medium for 8 minutes, stirring.
Add goat cheese and leeks.
Heat 'til combined.
Pour into 9 x 13 pan and cool.
Cut into wedges or rounds.
Proceed, Refrigerate, or Freeze.
(texture suffers when frozen)
Place on greased pan.
Bake at 400 for 10 minutes.
Top with Mango Mojo.
Reheat briefly.

Options: Top the polenta with Shiitake Mushrooms instead (see Shiitake Crostini).

Mango Mojo

(adapted from *Gourmet Magazine*)

1 mango, peeled and pitted
1 garlic, pressed
1 T rice wine vinegar
3 T lime juice
1 jalapeno, cut up with seeds
¼ t salt

Pulse mango to course chop.
Add garlic, vinegar, lime, jalapeno, and salt.

Pulse to fine chop.
(pureé if using as a dip)

Leek Polenta with Mango Mojo

Creamed Salmon with Chives on Mini-Biscuit Bites
makes 32 pieces or serves 2 for light dining

1 lb. salmon filet, cut in half

3 T butter
2 T flour
1 leek, minced
¼ t paprika
¼ t cayenne
1/8 t bay leaf, ground
1 ½ t fish stock base
¼ cup sherry
½ cup heavy cream
1 T lemon juice
¼ cup fresh chives, chopped

Boil enough water to cover salmon in one layer. Add salmon and cook on low for 8 minutes. Remove from water and cool.
Melt butter and cook flour on medium for 4 minutes. Add leek and cook on medium-low for 5 minutes.
Add paprika, cayenne, bay leaf, stock base, then sherry. Heat 'til smooth.

Add cream slowly, stirring 'til smooth. Add lemon juice then chives. Cool.
Pour off standing juice from salmon then flake. Moisten with just enough sauce to bind. Chill.

Mini-Biscuit Bites
makes 36 pieces or 6 large biscuits

1 stick butter, soft
8 oz. goat cheese, soft
1 ¼ cup flour (extra for rolling surface)
1 t salt

Combine butter and cheese.
Add flour and salt.
Mix and place on floured work surface.
Knead briefly 'til smooth.
Roll to ¼" thickness and make 1 ¼" biscuits.
Place on greased pan.
Bake at 450 for 10 minutes.
Spoon salmon onto biscuits.
Proceed, Refrigerate, or Freeze.
Bake at 300 for 5 minutes.

Grilled Tuna with Shallot Cream on Cornbread

Saffron Scallops with Cilantro Shallot Cream on Buttermilk Cornbread

makes 35 pieces

½ cup white wine
20 threads saffron (.2 g)
½ t fish stock base
½ lb. sea scallops, muscle removed, rinsed, and quartered

Heat wine and crumble in saffron.
Cook on low 5 minutes.
Add stock base then scallops.
Cook on low for 4 minutes.
Cool in broth.

4 oz. cream cheese, soft
3 oz. goat cheese, soft
1/8 t salt
¼ t cayenne
1 shallot, minced
¼ cup fresh cilantro, chopped

Mix cheeses with salt, cayenne, shallot, then cilantro.

1 cup flour
½ cup yellow cornmeal
1 t baking powder
1 T sugar
1 t salt
2 eggs
½ cup sour cream
¼ cup buttermilk
4 T butter, melted
1 cup white cheddar, grated

Combine flour, cornmeal, baking powder, sugar, and salt. Mix in eggs, sour cream, buttermilk, and butter.
Stir in cheddar.
Spread flat on 9 x 13 greased pan.
Bake at 375 for 16 minutes.
Cool and cut into 1" rounds.
Place cornbread on greased pan. Spoon or pipe on cheese mix.
Place scallop on cream.
Proceed, Refrigerate, or Freeze.

Bake at 300 for 5 minutes.

Option: Substitute tuna (see Seared Tuna Soft Tacos) for the scallops.

Red Onion Arepas with Mozzarella and Tomato

makes 50 pieces or serves 8 for light dining

3 T butter	Melt 3 T butter and cook onion on medium for 5 minutes.
1 red onion, minced	
1 t cumin	Add cumin and pepper.
1 t black pepper	
4 cups chicken stock	Boil liquid stock with butter.
(1 t base per 1 cup of water)	
4 T butter	
1 cup yellow cornmeal	Whisk in cornmeal and cook on medium-low for 10 minutes, stirring.
½ cup Parmesan, grated	Add Parmesan and onion mix.
	Heat 'til combined.
	Pour into 9 x 13 pan and cool.
	Cut out 1" stars.
	Proceed, Refrigerate, or Freeze.
	(texture suffers when frozen)
	Place stars on greased pan.
	Bake at 400 for 10 minutes to firm.
15 grape tomatoes, sliced	Top with tomato then cheese slice.
50 - ¾" square thin mozzarella slices	Bake at 350 for 5 minutes.
4 fresh sprigs cilantro	Top with cilantro leaf.

Garni: corn off the cob or sliced red onion on yellow bean threads
Options: Cut into wedges for light dining, and top with whole tomato slice and cheese.

Red Onion Arepas with Mozzarella and Tomato

Meat and Fish Nuggets
Toothpick Morsels

Ground Veal and Shallots in a Balsamic Vinegar Sauce

Lamb, Garlic, and Basil Nuggets in a Curried Red Pepper Pureé

Grilled Salmon Cakes with a Pineapple Salsa

Turkey Parmesan with Melted Mozzarella in a Spicy Marinara Sauce

African Lamb Babotie with Nutmeg Custard

Spicy Pork and Garlic Sausage in a Saffron Lime Sauce

Crab Cakes with Mustard Sauce

Beef Tenderloin with Béarnaise Sauce

Ginger, Jalapeno, and Yogurt Tandoori Chicken with a
Thai Peanut Dip

Tupelo Honey Scallops in a Chipotle Lime Hollandaise

Jamaican Jerk Pork in a Saffron Sauce
with Pink Peppercorn Olives

Ground Veal and Shallots in a Balsamic Vinegar Sauce

makes 50 pieces (25 meatballs halved)

½ lb. white mushrooms
3 T butter
5 shallots, minced
½ t thyme, powdered
2 garlic, pressed
1 ½ t black pepper
½ cup Marsala wine
1 T veal or chicken stock base
1 lb. ground veal
3 eggs
½ cup Romano cheese, grated
½ cup panko bread crumbs
½ cup fresh flat parsley, chopped
1 T fresh sage, minced

Pulse mushrooms 'til minced.
Melt butter and cook shallots on medium for 5 minutes.
Add thyme, garlic, black pepper, Marsala, and mushrooms.
Cook on medium-high 'til very moist.
Thoroughly mix in stock base.
Cook on medium 'til moist.
Combine veal, eggs, cheese, panko, parsley, sage, and mushrooms.
Form 1 ½" meatballs with cold, wet hands. (These will be halved, so be generous).
Heat oil and cook on medium-high for 2 minutes each side. Drain on paper towel.
Chill.
Proceed, Refrigerate, or Freeze.
Halve nuggets and place on greased pan, flat side down. Insert toothpicks.
Bake at 350 for 5 minutes.
Place in a pool of warm sauce.

Port Balsamic Vinegar Sauce

1 stick butter
5 shallots, minced
1 cup balsamic vinegar
2 cups port
1 T veal stock base
½ cup blackcurrant preserves (Chiver's)
1 T fresh sage, minced
1 T fresh rosemary, minced

Melt butter and cook shallots on medium for 5 minutes.
Add vinegar and reduce on medium-high 'til syrupy.
Add port and reduce on high by half.
Add stock base.
Add currant then briefly pulse with hand mixer to emulsify. Add sage and rosemary.
Warm to combine thoroughly.
Proceed, Refrigerate, or Freeze.

Lamb and Basil Nuggets in a Red Pepper Pureé

Lamb, Garlic, and Basil Nuggets in a Curried Red Pepper Pureé

makes 30 pieces (15 meatballs halved)

3 T butter
4 garlic, pressed
¼ t thyme, powdered
¼ t bay leaf, powdered
1 ½ t black pepper
2 t veal or chicken stock base
1 lb. ground lamb
3 eggs
½ cup Parmesan, grated
½ cup fresh basil, chopped
1 cup panko bread crumbs
½ cup vegetable oil

Melt butter and warm garlic on low for 1 minute.
Add thyme, bay leaf, pepper, and stock base. Mix thoroughly.

Combine lamb, eggs, herb butter, Parmesan, basil, and bread crumbs.
Form 1 ½" meatballs with cold, wet hands. (These will be halved, so be generous).
Heat oil and cook on medium-high for 2 minutes each side.
Drain on paper towel. Chill.
Proceed, Refrigerate, or Freeze.
Halve nuggets and place on greased pan, flat side down. Insert toothpicks.
Bake at 350 for 5 minutes.
Place in a pool of warm sauce.

Curried Red Pepper Pureé

½ stick butter
1 onion, chopped
2 jalapenos, chopped with seeds
4 red peppers, chopped
1 T chicken or vegetable stock base
1/8 t cayenne
1 T paprika
2 T curry powder
½ cup heavy cream

Melt butter and cook onion, jalapenos, and red peppers on medium for 10 minutes, covered.
Add stock base, cayenne, paprika, and curry. Warm on low for 1 minute. Pureé in blender.
Add cream.

Grilled Salmon Cakes with Pineapple Salsa

makes 25 pieces or serves 3 for light dining

1 lb. salmon filet
1 T vegetable oil
½ t adobo seasoning

Roll salmon in oil and season with adobo.
Grill over medium coals for 4 minutes each side.
Chill. Flake.

3 T butter, melted
3 eggs
2 T spicy brown mustard
2 T lemon juice
1/8 t cayenne
½ t salt
1 shallot, minced
4 scallions, minced
¼ cup fresh flat parsley, chopped
1 cup panko bread crumbs
2 cups panko bread crumbs
2 T fresh dill, chopped
3 eggs
½ cup vegetable oil

Mix butter, eggs, mustard, lemon, cayenne, and salt. Add shallot, scallions, parsley, 1 cup panko, and salmon.
Chill 2 hours...better yet overnight.

Mix 2 cups panko with dill.
Beat 3 eggs in separate bowl.
Make 1" salmon cakes with cold, wet hands.
Dip in egg. Lift out and roll in panko.
Heat oil and cook on medium-high for 2 minutes each side. Press in one side slightly to hold salsa. Drain on paper towels.
Proceed, Refrigerate, or Freeze.
Bake at 450 for 5 minutes.
Place salsa on each cake.

Pineapple Salsa

½ cup fresh pineapple, minced
½ yellow pepper, minced
1 jalapeno, no seeds, minced
½ red onion, minced
1 T lime juice
2 T rice wine vinegar
1 t sugar

Combine all ingredients.
Place in zip baggie, press out air, and seal.
Chill for 3 hours.
Lift salsa from juice when serving.

Grilled Salmon Cakes with Pineapple Salsa on Asian Seaweed

Turkey Parmesan with Melted Mozzarella in a Spicy Marinara Sauce

makes 40 pieces (20 meatballs halved)

3 T butter 3 shallots, minced	Melt butter and cook shallots on medium for 5 minutes.
¼ t oregano, ground ¼ t bay leaf, ground 1 ½ t black pepper 2 garlic, pressed 2 t chicken stock base ¼ t hickory smoke flavoring	Add oregano, bay leaf, pepper, garlic, stock base, and hickory flavoring. Mix thoroughly.
1 lb. ground turkey 3 eggs ½ cup Parmesan, grated ½ cup fresh basil, chopped 1 cup panko bread crumbs	Mix turkey, eggs, Parmesan, basil, and panko with shallot mix. Form 1 ½" meatballs with cold, wet hands. (These will be halved, so be generous).
½ cup vegetable oil	Heat oil and cook on medium-high for 2 minutes each side. Drain on paper towel. Chill. Proceed, Refrigerate, or Freeze.
	Halve turkey nuggets and place cut side down on greased pan.
8 slices mozzarella, cut in 1" squares	
	Top with mozzarella and insert toothpick. Bake at 350 for 5 minutes. Place in a pool of warm sauce.

Spicy Marinara Sauce
(adapted from Armida's recipe)

½ cup light olive oil	Warm oil and heat garlic on low for 5 minutes.
8 garlic, pressed	Remove and discard garlic.
1 t red pepper flakes	Add pepper flakes, onion, and sugar.
1 onion, minced	Cook on medium for 5 minutes.
3 T sugar	
6 oz. can tomato paste	Add tomato paste and cook 5 minutes.
56 oz. peeled Italian plum tomatoes	Food mill tomatoes (with liquid).
¼ t bay leaf, ground	Add to paste with bay leaf, basil, salt, pepper, and 1 cup water.
¼ t dried basil, crumbled	
1 t salt	
½ t black pepper	
	Cook on medium for 30 minutes...better yet 1 hour.

Garni: orange pepper strips, halved tomato for used toothpicks
Options: This marinara's great on pasta too. It freezes very well.

African Lamb Babotie with Nutmeg Custard

African Lamb Babotie with Nutmeg Custard

(adapted from the recipe of Ann Sargent)
makes 80 pieces or serves 6 for light dining

1 T light olive oil 2 lbs. lamb, trimmed and ground	Heat 1 T oil and cook lamb on medium for 10 minutes 'til crumbly, breaking apart. Pour off most fat. Cool.
2 T light olive oil 2 onions, minced 2 T curry ¼ t tumeric ¼ t bay leaf, ground 2 T white vinegar 1 T sugar 2 t chicken stock base 1 T black pepper	In separate pan, heat 2 T oil and cook onions on medium for 5 minutes. Add curry, tumeric, bay leaf, vinegar, sugar, stock base, and pepper. Cool.
¾ c milk 10 slices white bread, crust removed 3 eggs 2 egg yolks 1/3 cup raisins 3 T chutney 1 lemon zest, minced ¾ cups panko bread crumbs	Pour ¾ cup milk over white bread and mash. Add eggs, yolks, raisins, chutney, lemon zest, panko, then onions and meat. Press flat into greased 9 x 13 pan, and cover tightly with foil. Bake at 350 for 1 hour 15 minutes.
3 eggs ¼ t nutmeg ¾ c milk ½ c heavy cream ¼ t salt	Mix 3 eggs, nutmeg, milk, cream, and salt. When meat is cooked, pour custard on top and bake, uncovered, at 300 for 25 minutes. Chill in pan. Cut into wedges. Place on greased pan. Proceed, Refrigerate, or Freeze. Bake at 450 for 5 minutes.

Spicy Pork Sausage in a Saffron Lime Sauce

makes 40 pieces (20 meatballs halved)

3 T butter
3 garlic, pressed
¼ t oregano, powdered
1/8 t bay leaf, powdered
½ t cayenne
1 t black pepper
½ t paprika
2 t chicken stock base
1 lb. ground pork
3 eggs
½ cup Parmesan, grated
1 cup panko bread crumbs
½ cup fresh basil, chopped
½ cup vegetable oil

Melt butter and warm garlic on low for 1 minute.
Add oregano, bay leaf, cayenne, pepper, paprika, and stock base.
Warm to combine.
Mix pork, eggs, cheese, panko, herb butter, and basil.
Form 1 ½" meatballs with cold, wet hands. (These will be halved, so be generous).
Heat oil and cook on medium-high for 2 minutes each side.
Drain on paper towel. Chill.
Proceed, Refrigerate, or Freeze.
Halve nuggets and place on greased pan, flat side down. Insert toothpicks.
Bake at 350 for 5 minutes.
Place in a pool of warm sauce.

Saffron Lime Sauce

2 T lime juice
40 threads saffron (.4g)

2 sticks butter
2 T milk solids or ¼ t salt
(see Cooking Notes)
4 egg yolks
3 T lime juice

¼ cup heavy cream

Zap lime for 20 seconds.
Crumble saffron into it.
Zap another 10 seconds.
Let sit for 15 minutes.
Heat butter and milk solids to full boil.
Combine egg yolks and lime.
Zap 10 seconds, stir. Repeat.
With hand mixer (or blender), slowly add ¾ of butter to eggs in steady stream.
Add saffron and cream to loosen.
Blend 'til smooth adding remaining butter, scraping bottom of pan.

Spicy Pork Sausage in a Saffron Lime Sauce

Crab Cakes with Mustard Sauce

makes 30 pieces or serves 5 for light dining

3 T butter	Melt butter and cook shallots and red pepper on medium for 8 minutes.
2 shallots, minced	
½ red pepper, minced and squeezed dry in paper towels	
1 garlic, pressed	Add garlic, lemon zest, and stock base.
½ lemon zest, minced	Mix thoroughly. Cool.
1 ½ t fish stock base	
2 eggs plus 1 egg yolk	Mix eggs, Dijon, lemon, Worcestershire, cayenne, and red pepper mix. Mix in crab and 1 ½ cups panko.
1 T Dijon	
1 T lemon juice	
1 T Worcestershire	Chill 2 hours...better yet overnight.
¼ t cayenne	
2 lbs. fresh crab leg only, picked over	
1 ½ cups panko bread crumbs	
2 cups panko bread crumbs	Mix 2 cups panko with pepper and parsley. Form 1" crab cakes and roll in panko, pressing crumbs into crab cake.
½ t black pepper	
1 T fresh flat parsley, chopped	
	Lay out in single layer. Chill 1 hour.
1 cup vegetable oil	Heat oil and cook crab cakes on medium for 1 minute each side. Drain on paper towel. Proceed, Refrigerate, or Freeze.
	Bake at 450 for 5 minutes. Let sit a bit then serve with dipping sauce.

Mustard Sauce

2 T lemon juice	Mix lemon, mustard, curry, sugar, and salt.
3 T dry mustard	
1 T curry powder	
3 T sugar	
1 t salt	
½ cup Hellman's mayo	Mix mayo and sour cream.
½ cup sour cream	Add to spices.
	Chill 4 hours...minimum!

Beef Tenderloin with Béarnaise Sauce

makes 35 pieces or serves 2 for light dining

1 lb. beef tenderloin, cut in 1" pieces	Toss beef in oil.
2 T vegetable oil	Spread in single layer.
½ t salt	Evenly season beef with salt, onion, garlic, and pepper. Toss.
½ t onion powder	
½ t garlic powder	Chill in baggie for 2 (up to 24) hours.
½ t black pepper	

Place beef in pan large enough to hold in single layer.
Broil 3 minutes.
Insert toothpicks and place in a pool of warm sauce.

Béarnaise Sauce

Reduction:
3 shallots, minced
1 t sugar
3 T dried tarragon, crumbled
1 cup white wine vinegar

Combine shallots, sugar, tarragon, and vinegar.
Cook on med-high 'til very moist.

4 egg yolks
3 T lemon juice
2 sticks butter
3 T milk solids (or ¼ t salt)
(see Cooking Notes)
¼ cup heavy cream
yellow food color

Mix egg yolks and lemon.
Zap 10 seconds. Stir. Repeat.
Heat butter and milk solids to full boil.
With hand mixer (or blender), slowly add ¾ of butter to eggs in a steady stream. Blend in cream to loosen.
Blend in remaining butter, scraping pan. Add 2 T tarragon reduction.
Add 2 drops yellow food color.
Reheat on low, stirring.

Garni: cranberries or asparagus, halved lemon for used toothpicks.

Ginger Tandoori Chicken with a Thai Peanut Dip
makes 75 pieces or serves 5 for light dining

3 T lime juice 2 T cornstarch	Mix lime and cornstarch.
2 garlic, pressed 2 jalapenos, minced with seeds 2 T fresh ginger, minced 1 T paprika ¼ t tumeric 1 T cumin 1 T salt 2 T vegetable oil ½ cup yogurt	Add garlic, jalapeno, ginger, paprika, tumeric, cumin, salt, oil, and yogurt.
3 lbs. chicken breast, boneless and skinless	Cut chicken into bite-sized pieces. Toss in sauce and chill overnight.
3 T vegetable oil	Coat pan with oil. Add chicken in a single layer. Bake at 375 for 10 minutes, stirring after 5 minutes. Insert toothpick and serve with warm dip.

Thai Peanut Dip

¾ c rice vinegar ½ c water 2 T sugar	Heat vinegar, water, and sugar on high for 1 minute to dissolve sugar.
1 cup unsalted roasted peanuts 1" fresh ginger, peeled 1 garlic, pressed 2 t red pepper flakes	Process peanuts, ginger, garlic, and pepper 'til finely chopped. Add half vinegar mixture and process 1 minute. Add remaining vinegar and process 1 minute more 'til very smooth.
2 T sesame oil	Add sesame and process.

Tupelo Honey Scallops in a Chipotle Lime Hollandaise

makes 24 pieces or serves 2 for light dining

1 lb. sea scallops	Remove muscle if attached to side of scallop, rinse, and drain.
	Halve if bigger than 1 ½".
1 T vegetable oil	Mix oil, chipotle sauce, and honey.
1 T chipotle sauce (see Grilled Chicken Quesadillas)	
1 T Tupelo honey	Add scallops.
	Lay in pan in single layer.
	Broil for 6 minutes, stirring halfway.
	Let sit 5 minutes. Drain.
	Insert toothpicks.
	Place in a pool of warm sauce.

Chipotle Lime Hollandaise

4 egg yolks	Mix egg yolks and lime.
3 T lime juice	Zap 10 seconds. Stir. Repeat.
2 sticks butter	Heat butter and milk solids to full boil.
3 T milk solids or ¼ t salt (see Cooking Notes)	With hand mixer (or blender), slowly add ¾ of butter to eggs in a steady stream.
¼ cup heavy cream	Blend in cream to loosen.
2 T chipotle sauce	Blend in remaining butter, scraping pan.
¼ cup fresh cilantro, chopped	Blend in chipotle sauce then cilantro.
	Reheat on low, stirring.

Garni: grape tomatoes, whole jalapenos, halved orange for used toothpicks
Note: You may substitute clover honey, but it won't sound as interesting.
Options: Don't cut scallops for light dining, but cook for 7 minutes then toss in sauce.

Jamaican Jerk Pork in a Saffron Sauce with Pink Peppercorn Olives
(adapted from Gourmet Magazine)
makes 30 pieces or serves 2 for light dining

½ sweet onion, grated	Discard most liquid from onion then mix wet pulp with stock base.
1 t chicken stock base	
¼ t thyme, ground	Add thyme, sugar, black pepper, cayenne, nutmeg, allspice, and cinnamon.
1 t sugar	
½ t black pepper	
¼ t cayenne	
½ t nutmeg	
1/8 t allspice	
1/8 t cinnamon	Remove all fat and blue skin from pork. Cut into 1" pieces.
1 lb. pork tenderloin	
	Toss in spices.
	Chill 1 hour…better yet overnight.
	Pour oil in pan large enough to hold pork in single layer. Toss pork in oil.
¼ cup vegetable oil	
	Broil for 6 minutes, stirring halfway.
Saffron Lime Sauce	Insert toothpicks.
(see Spicy Pork Sausage)	Place in a pool of warm saffron sauce.

Pink Peppercorn Olives
(adapted from the recipe of Jennifer Campo)

2 cups mixed olives, drained and pitted	Toss all ingredients in a zip baggie. Press out air, seal, and chill overnight.
3 T virgin olive oil	
2 garlic, smashed intact	
½ orange peel, cut in thick strips, saving other half	Discard garlic and replace discolored orange before serving in a bowl on the platter. A halved blood orange is a great used toothpick holder.
½ t fresh rosemary, minced plus 3 sprigs	
½ t red pepper flakes	
1 t pink peppercorns	

Quesadillas and Tortillas

Roquefort, Merlot Apple, and Walnut Quesadillas with Cardamom Applesauce

Seared Tuna Soft Tacos with Jalapenos

Grilled Chicken and Chipotle Pepper Quesadillas

Shrimp, Feta, and Arugula Quesadillas with Lime

Mushroom Quesadillas with Marsala and Basil

Black Bean Nachos with Avocado, Cheddar, and Sour Cream

BBQ Beef and Sage Quesadillas

Cactus Quesadillas with Cilantro

Roquefort, Walnut, and Apple Quesadillas with Cardamom Applesauce and Spiced Pecans

Roquefort Quesadillas with Cardamom Applesauce

makes 50 pieces or serves 5 for light dining

1 cup merlot wine
2 T lemon
4 T sugar
1 t nutmeg
½ t cinnamon
½ t cloves
2 apples, peeled and chopped
1 cup walnuts, roasted and chopped

2 cups white cheddar, grated
½ cup Parmesan, grated
6 oz. Roquefort, well crumbled
1 ½ t black pepper
1 T lemon juice
3 T flat parsley, chopped
10 flour tortillas, fajita 8" size

½ cup vegetable oil

Heat wine, lemon, sugar, nutmeg, cinnamon, and clove.
Add apples and cook on medium 'til quite soft – about 8 minutes.
Chill in juice.

Bake walnuts at 350 for 10 minutes.
Chop.
Mix cheddar, Parmesan, Roquefort, pepper, walnuts, lemon, drained apples, then parsley.
Lay out 5 tortillas.
Mound 1 generous cup of filling on each, leaving 1" edge.
Press another tortilla firmly on top.
Heat skillet adding oil to cover bottom.
Cook quesadilla on medium for 1 minute.
Flip by turning it over onto your hand (cool side down), then let it slide back onto the skillet.
Cook 1 minute more.
Drain on paper towels and press filling to edge.
Chill.
Slice each quesadilla into 10 wedges.
Proceed, Refrigerate, or Freeze.
Lay wedges on baking pan protected by foil (in case cheese melts a bit).
Heat at 300 for 5 minutes.

Cardamom Applesauce

8 oz. Mott's applesauce
¼ t cardamom
1 drop red food coloring

Mix applesauce, cardamom, and food coloring.
Chill.

Seared Tuna Soft Tacos with Jalapenos

makes 16 large pieces or serves 4 for light dining

½ cup Hellman's mayo
1 T lime juice
1 T Hidden Valley Ranch Mix
1/8 t cayenne
1 sweet onion, grated and squeezed dry
3 T sour cream
2 jalapenos, no seeds, chopped
¼ cup fresh cilantro, chopped

Stir mayo, add lime, then ranch mix.

Add cayenne, onion, sour cream, jalapenos, and cilantro.
Chill for 4 hours.

1 t black pepper
½ t sugar
1 t adobo seasoning
1 lb. fresh tuna, cut into 1" thick steaks

Combine pepper, sugar, and adobo. Season both sides of tuna.

Grill over hot coals on a well-oiled rack for 2 minutes each side 'til rare. Cool. Proceed or Refrigerate.

8 flour tortillas, fajita size or 8"

Cut tuna into thin slices against the grain.
Lay out tortillas and place tuna strip across bottom third of tortilla.
Cover with 2 T dressing. Roll up.
Place seam side down on cookie sheet large enough to hold all tacos snugly.
Chill for 4 hours, covered.

Cover with wax paper.
Bake at 300 for 10 minutes. Halve.

Garni: broccoli or asparagus and grape tomatoes
Note: You'll want cocktail plates with these.

Grilled Chicken and Chipotle Pepper Quesadillas
makes 60 pieces or serves 6 for light dining

1 T vegetable oil
1 t cornstarch
1 t adobo seasoning
½ t black pepper
1 ½ lbs. chicken thighs, boneless and skinless
2 T chipotle seasoning (below)
1/8 t cayenne
3 T lime juice
3 cups white cheddar, grated
¼ cup Parmesan, grated
½ cup fresh cilantro, chopped
12 flour tortillas, fajita-size
½ cup vegetable oil

Mix cornstarch in oil.
Add adobo and pepper.
Coat chicken and let sit 15 minutes. Grill on medium-high for 4 minutes each side. Chill.
Mix chipotle sauce, cayenne, and lime.
Add to cheddar and Parmesan.
Finely chop chicken. Add to cheese with cilantro. Lay out 6 tortillas.
Mound 1 generous cup of filling on each, leaving 1" edge.
Press another tortilla firmly on top.
Heat skillet adding oil to cover bottom.
Cook quesadilla on medium for 1 minute.
Flip by turning it over onto your hand then let it slide back onto the skillet. Cook 1 minute more.
Drain on paper towels and press filling to edge.
Chill.
Slice each quesadilla into 10 wedges.
Proceed, Refrigerate, or Freeze.
Lay wedges on baking pan protected by foil (in case cheese melts a bit).
Bake at 300 for 5 minutes.

8 oz. hot red salsa
1 T ketchup

Combine salsa and ketchup.
Serve with red salsa as dip.

Chipotle Sauce

4 garlic, pressed
7 oz. can chipotle peppers in adobo
3 T balsamic vinegar
1 T cumin
4 T Tupelo or clover honey
3 T spicy brown mustard
2 t salt

Process garlic and peppers.
Add remaining ingredients and pureé.

Shrimp, Feta, and Arugula Quesadillas with Lime

makes 50 pieces or serves 5 for light dining

¾ lb. cooked shrimp, tail off	Pulse shrimp to coarse chop. Reserve.
8 oz. feta	Pulse feta 'til crumbled then add to shrimp.

1 ½ cups white cheddar, grated	Mix cheddar, Parmesan, salsa, and lime.
¼ cup Parmesan, grated	Add shrimp then arugula.
6 oz. hot verde salsa (green)	
2 T lime juice	
1 cup arugula, chopped	

10 flour tortillas, fajita 8" size	Lay out 5 tortillas.
	Mound 1 generous cup of filling on each, leaving 1" edge.
	Press another tortilla firmly on top.
½ cup vegetable oil	Heat skillet adding oil to cover bottom.
	Cook quesadilla on medium for 1 minute.
	Flip by turning it over onto your hand, then let it slide back onto the skillet. Cook 1 minute more.
	Drain on paper towels and press filling to edge.
	Chill.
	Slice each quesadilla into 10 wedges.
	Proceed, Refrigerate, or Freeze.

	Lay wedges on baking pan protected by foil (in case cheese melts a bit).
	Heat at 300 for 5 minutes.
8 oz. hot verde salsa, for dip	Serve with green salsa as dip.

Garni: orange pepper strips on dark olive bean threads

Mushroom Quesadillas with Marsala and Basil

makes 60 pieces or serves 6 for light dining

2 T butter	Melt butter and heat garlic on low for
4 garlic, pressed	1 minute.
1/8 t bay leaf, ground	Add bay leaf, thyme, black pepper, Marsala,
¼ t thyme, ground	and white mushrooms.
1 T black pepper	Cook on medium-high 'til very moist.
½ cup dry Marsala or sherry	
8 oz. white mushrooms, chopped	
1 T mushroom stock base	Mix in stock base then add shiitakes.
4 oz. shiitake mushrooms, chopped	Cook on low for 4 minutes. Cool.
½ cup Parmesan, grated	Mix mushrooms with Parmesan.
3 cups white cheddar, grated	Add cheddar and basil.
½ cup fresh basil, chopped	
12 flour tortillas, fajita-size or 8"	Lay out 6 tortillas.
	Mound 1 generous cup of filling on each, leaving 1" edge.
	Press another tortilla firmly on top.
½ cup vegetable oil	Heat skillet adding oil to cover bottom.
	Cook quesadilla on medium for 1 minute.
	Flip by turning it over onto your hand then let it slide back onto the skillet. Cook 1 minute more.
	Drain on paper towels and press filling to edge.
	Chill.
	Slice each quesadilla into 10 wedges.
	Proceed, Refrigerate, or Freeze.
	Lay wedges on baking pan protected by foil (in case cheese melts a bit).
	Heat at 300 for 4 minutes.
8 oz. hot red salsa	Combine salsa and ketchup.
1 T ketchup	Serve with red salsa as dip.

Black Bean Nachos

Black Bean Nachos with Avocado and Sour Cream

(adapted from Memories of a Cuban Kitchen – Randelman)
makes 30 pieces or serves 8 for beans for light dining

1 cup dried black beans	Rinse beans then soak overnight.
1 green pepper, chopped	Don't drain, adding more water to cover beans by 2".
¼ t bay leaf, ground	Add pepper and bay leaf.
½ cup virgin olive oil	Boil then simmer for 2 hours, uncovered, adding water as needed to cover beans.
1 onion, chopped	Heat oil and cook onion and pepper on medium-low for 8 minutes.
1 green pepper, chopped	Add garlic, chilies, cumin, and vinegar.
4 garlic, pressed	Add to beans and cook on low, covered, for 45 minutes.
2 T green chilies(can), chopped	
1 T cumin	
2 T apple cider vinegar	
	Add cayenne, salt, and pepper.
¼ t cayenne	Let cool 10 minutes.
2 t salt	Lift 2 cups beans from liquid and process beans with enough liquid to a smooth, thick pureé.
2 t black pepper	Cool.
	Lay tortillas on pan and pipe or spoon on bean pureé. Sprinkle with cheese and top with tomato.
1 bag lime tostitos	Proceed or Refrigerate.
½ cup white cheddar, grated	Mash avocado to pureé.
8 grape tomatoes, quartered	Add lime and salt.
	Place in baggie, cutting off small corner to make a pastry bag.
1 ripe avocado	
1 T lime	
¼ t salt	
½ cup sour cream	Place sour cream in baggie, cutting off small corner to make a pastry bag.
	Broil nachos for 2-3 minutes.
	Pipe on avocado and sour cream.

Bourbon BBQ Beef and Sage Quesadillas

(adapted from Burning Passions – W. Park Kerr)

makes 50 pieces or serves 5 for light dining

1 flat beef brisket (2-3 lbs.)	Combine all herbs and rub into beef.
1 t cumin	Chill overnight.
1 t chili powder	Make barbecue sauce (next page).
1 t sugar	Prepare grill with charcoal piled at ends.
1 t salt	Soak hickory chips in water 15 minutes.
1 t black pepper	Lay 1 cup of drained chips on hot coals.
1 t oregano, dried	Place beef in center of grill.
1 t onion powder	Cover with ½ cup barbecue sauce.
1 t paprika	Cover grill. Smoke for as long as smoke lasts, about ½ hour. Add remaining hickory to coals,
2 cups hickory chips, for smoking	flip beef, and cover with ½ cup sauce. Cook ½ hour.
1 beer	Line roasting pan with enough foil to encase beef. Add beef and beer. Close tightly and bake at 300 for 3 ½ hours. Cool. Chill in juices.
	Cut beef in chunks and pulse to shred.
1 shallot, minced	Add shallot, jalapeno, and sage to combine.
2 jalapenos, minced with seeds	Moisten 4 cups of beef with 1 cup barbecue
½ cup fresh sage, minced	sauce to bind. Add cheese.
3 cups white cheddar, grated	
10 flour tortillas, fajita 8" size	Lay out 5 tortillas.
	Mound 1 generous cup of filling on each, leaving 1" edge.
	Press another tortilla firmly on top.
½ cup vegetable oil	Heat skillet adding oil to cover bottom.
	Cook quesadilla on medium for 1 minute.
	Flip by turning it over onto your hand, then let it slide back onto the skillet. Cook 1 minute more.
	Drain on paper towels and press filling to edge. Chill.
	Slice each quesadilla into 10 wedges.
	Proceed, Refrigerate, or Freeze.
	Lay wedges on baking pan protected by foil (in case cheese melts a bit).
	Heat at 300 for 5 minutes.
	Serve with barbecue sauce as dip.

Bourbon BBQ Sauce

22 oz. hickory barbecue sauce
¼ cup bourbon
1 T apple cider vinegar
2 t chili powder
¼ t cayenne

Combine sauce, bourbon, vinegar, chili powder, and cayenne.
Boil. Chill.

Cactus Quesadillas with Cilantro
makes 50 pieces or serves 5 for light dining

1 cup cactus strips (jar), rinsed, picked over, and drained overnight
4 oz. hot verde salsa (green)
½ cup Parmesan, grated
1 T lime juice

Chop cactus and mix with salsa, Parmesan, and lime.

3 cups white cheddar, grated
½ cup fresh cilantro, chopped

Add cheddar then cilantro.

10 flour tortillas, fajita size or 8"

Lay out 5 tortillas.
Mound 1 generous cup of filling on each, leaving 1" edge.
Press another tortilla firmly on top.

½ cup vegetable oil

Heat skillet adding oil to cover bottom.
Cook quesadilla on medium for 1 minute.
Flip by turning it over onto your hand, then let it slide back onto the skillet. Cook 1 minute more.
Drain on paper towels and press filling to edge.
Chill.
Slice each quesadilla into 10 wedges.
Proceed, Refrigerate, or Freeze.

Lay wedges on baking pan protected by foil (in case cheese melts a bit).

8 oz. hot red salsa
1 T ketchup

Heat at 300 for 5 minutes.
Combine salsa and ketchup.
Serve with red salsa as dip.

Garni: green beans

Crostini and Frittata

Gruyere Scallop Crostini with Dill

Shrimp, Jalapeno, and Goat Cheese Crostini

Pistachio, Cilantro, and Jalapeno Bruschetta
with Marinated Tomatoes

Eggplant and Oregano or Shiitake Mushrooms with
St. André Cheese Crostini

Poached Pear, Brie, and Pommery Crostini

Cuttlefish Ink Frittata with Leeks and Smoked Salmon

Artichoke, Habanero, and Basil Crostini

Olive, Arugula, and Habanero Frittata

Gruyere Scallop Crostini

Gruyere Scallop Crostini with Dill

(adapted from the recipe of Cathie Walsh)
makes 30 pieces or serves 2 for light dining

2 T butter	Melt butter then add lemon zest and garlic.
1 lemon zest, minced	Warm on low for 1 minute.
2 garlic, pressed	
1 lb. sea scallops, muscle removed, rinsed, and chopped	Add scallops and flour and cook on medium-high for 4 minutes, stirring.
1 T flour	
1 T fresh dill, chopped	Add dill and cool.
	Discard 2 T standing liquid from pan.
¾ cup Hellman's mayo	Stir mayo and add Gruyere and pepper.
¾ cup Gruyere, grated	Combine scallops with mayo. Chill.
1 t black pepper	
6 finger rolls, not crusty	Slice rolls ½" thick discarding irregular ends.
1 stick butter, clarified	Dip one side in butter and lay on greased pan, butter side up.
(see Cooking Notes)	Place mound of scallops on crostini.
	Proceed, Refrigerate, or Freeze.
	Bake at 450 for 5 minutes.

Garni: asparagus or pale blue bean threads with cranberries
Options: For light dining, bake scallop mix in casserole at 300 for 25 minutes.

Shrimp, Jalapeno, and Goat Cheese Crostini
makes 36 pieces

5 T butter	Melt butter and cook flour on medium-low for 4 minutes, stirring.
2 T flour	Cool slightly.
¼ t bay leaf, ground	Add bay leaf, stock base, lemon zest, jalapenos, and garlic.
1 t fish stock base	
1 lemon zest, minced	Heat on low for 1 minute.
2 jalapenos, chopped with seeds	
2 garlic, pressed	
¼ cup white wine	Stir in wine, then cream.
½ cup heavy cream	Heat 'til smooth.
6 oz. goat cheese	Add goat cheese and warm to blend.
1 lb. cooked shrimp, chopped	Add shrimp, lime, cheddar, then cilantro.
1 T lime juice	
½ cup cheddar, grated	
½ cup fresh cilantro, chopped	
6 finger rolls	Slice rolls ½" thick discarding irregular ends.
1 stick butter, clarified	Dip one side in butter and lay on greased pan, butter side up.
(see Cooking Notes)	Top with shrimp mix.
	Proceed, Refrigerate, or Freeze.
	Bake at 450 for 5 minutes.

Garni: whole jalapenos and red pepper strips

Pistachio, Cilantro, and Jalapeno Bruschetta with Marinated Tomatoes

(adapted from *Bon Appetit Magazine*)
makes 30 pieces or serves 6 for light dining

2 garlic, pressed	Process garlic, salt, and lime zest. Add pistachios and process to fine mince.
½ t salt	
1 lime zest	
½ cup shelled pistachios	
2 cups fresh cilantro	Add cilantro, parsley, and jalapenos. Process almost to pureé.
½ cup fresh flat parsley	
2 jalapenos, mostly seeded and cut	
½ cup light olive oil plus 1 T	With machine running, slowly add ½ cup oil or enough to make thick pureé. Transfer to container pouring 1 T oil on surface. Chill overnight.
5 plum tomatoes	Chop tomatoes evenly, salt, and drain in colander for 15 minutes.
¼ t salt	
6 finger rolls, not crusty	Slice rolls ½" thick discarding irregular ends.
1 stick butter, clarified (see Cooking Notes)	Dip one side in butter and lay on greased pan, butter side up.
1 T red wine vinegar	In bowl, toss tomatoes in vinegar. Place a dollop of pesto on each crostini. Top with a few tomatoes.
Asiago, for grating	Grate Asiago on top. Proceed, Refrigerate, or Freeze. Bake at 450 for 5 minutes.

Options: Substitute basil for the cilantro.
Use larger, thicker bread slice for light dining, pile on the toppings, bake for 10 minutes, then drizzle with a fine olive oil.

Eggplant and Oregano or Shiitake Mushrooms with St. André Cheese Crostini

makes 30 pieces

3 T butter
3 garlic, pressed
1/8 t bay leaf, ground
1/8 t thyme, ground
1 t black pepper
½ cup dry Marsala wine
1 ½ t mushroom stock base
½ lb. shiitakes, thinly sliced
½ cup fresh basil, chopped

Melt butter.
Heat garlic on low for 1 minute.
Add bay leaf, thyme, black pepper, and Marsala. Cook on med-low for 5 minutes 'til very moist. Mix in stock base.
Add mushrooms and cook 2 minutes. Cool, add basil, then chill.

ALTERNATE TOPPING:
1 peeled eggplant, evenly chopped
½ t salt
1 T olive oil
2 garlic, pressed
¼ t powdered oregano
½ t black pepper

Sprinkle eggplant with salt. Stir.
Let sit in colander for 30 minutes.
Heat oil and warm garlic on low for 1 minute.
Add oregano and pepper.
Add eggplant and cook on med-high for 2 minutes. Chill.

4 oz. St. André cheese, rind removed
4 oz. cream cheese, soft
½ sweet onion, grated and squeezed dry
1 T lemon juice
pinch salt
6 finger rolls, not crusty
1 stick butter, clarified
(see Cooking Notes)

Puree St. André in processor with cream cheese, onion, lemon, and salt.
Chill to firm.

Slice rolls ½" thick discarding irregular ends.
Dip one side in butter and lay on greased pan, butter side up.
Pipe or spread cream cheese on crostini then top with mushrooms or eggplant.
Proceed, Refrigerate, or Freeze.
Bake at 450 for 5 minutes.

Shiitake Mushroom Crostini with Portabellas

Poached Pear and Brie Crostini

Poached Pear, Brie, and Pommery Crostini
makes 30 pieces

½ cup each red and white wine
2 T lemon juice
4 T sugar
½ t nutmeg
½ t cinnamon
½ t clove

Heat wines, lemon, sugar, nutmeg, cinnamon, and clove.

2 pears, thinly sliced (larger slices halved to fit on crostini)

Add pears and cook on low 'til barely softened – about 10 minutes.
Chill in juice.

6 finger rolls, not crusty
1 stick butter, clarified
(see Cooking Notes)

Slice rolls ½" thick discarding irregular ends.
Dip one side in butter and lay on greased pan, butter side up.

½ cup stone ground mustard
1 lb. Brie

Spread ½ t mustard on each crostini. Top with a thin slice of Brie.
Top with a slice of poached pear.
Proceed, Refrigerate, or Freeze.

Bake at 450 for 5 minutes.

Garni: red seedless grapes or purple mini-champagne grapes

Cuttlefish Ink Frittata with Smoked Salmon

Cuttlefish Ink Frittata with Leeks and Smoked Salmon

makes 40 pieces or serves 6 for light dining

1 cup sour cream	Drain sour cream in strainer overnight.
2 T lime juice	Zap lime for 20 seconds.
40 threads saffron (.4 g)	Crumble saffron into it.
1/8 t salt	Zap another 10 seconds.
	Let sit for 15 minutes.
	Combine with sour cream and salt.
	Chill.
2 red peppers, halved, stemmed, and seeded	Press peppers completely flat on pan, skin side up. Broil 'til black.
3 T light olive oil	Let sit 30 minutes.
3 garlic, smashed intact	Wipe off and discard blackened skin (rinse fingers but keep peppers dry). Cut peppers into thin strips.
½ t salt	
2 T butter	
3 leeks, white only, minced	Marinate in oil, garlic, and salt overnight.
1 t chicken stock base	Discard garlic and strain peppers, saving oil.
1 t habanero (jar), seeded and minced	Heat pepper oil with butter. Add leeks and cook on medium for 5 minutes. Add stock base, habanero, and roasted red peppers.
6 oz. black pasta (fettucine preferably)	Cook ink pasta in salted boiling water. Rinse in hot water and drain.
4 eggs	Combine all eggs with hot pasta and red pepper butter. Mix thoroughly.
4 eggbeaters	Add both cheeses then black beans.
½ lb. soft Italian Fontina, grated	
½ cup Parmesan, grated	
1 cup black beans (can), rinsed	Heat a 10" non-stick skillet on medium then butter lightly.
2 T butter for pan	Spread pasta mixture evenly.

8 oz. smoked salmon

Cook on low, centering flame under each quarter for 5 minutes – 20 minutes this side.
Off heat, place slightly larger platter over skillet and flip.
Push and slide frittata back onto re-buttered pan.
Again, move heat around edges and cook 15 minutes total this side.
Slide off, cool, then chill overnight.
Discard irregular edges, and cut into small wedges. Place on greased pan.
Proceed, Refrigerate, or Freeze.
Bake at 450 for 5 minutes.
Top with saffron cream and smoked salmon.

Options: Regular fettucine tastes great... simply less dramatic looking.

Artichoke, Habanero, and Basil Crostini
makes 30 pieces

2 T butter
2 shallots, peeled and minced
1/8 t ground thyme
1 t chicken stock base
½ t habanero pepper (jar), seeded and finely minced
1 can artichoke hearts (8 count total), rinsed, squeezed, and minced
3 oz. goat cheese
1 egg
¼ cup fresh basil, chopped
½ cup white cheddar, grated
6 finger rolls
1 stick butter, clarified
(see Cooking Notes)
Asiago Cheese, for grating

Heat butter and cook shallots on medium-low for 4 minutes.
Add thyme, stock base, habanero, artichokes, and goat cheese.
Heat to combine. Remove from heat.

Add egg, basil, then cheddar. Chill.

Slice rolls ½" thick discarding irregular ends.
Dip one side in butter and lay on greased pan, butter side up.
Mound artichoke mix on crostini.
Grate Asiago on top.
Proceed, Refrigerate, or Freeze.
Bake at 450 for 5 minutes.

Olive, Arugula, and Habanero Frittata

makes 40 pieces or serves 4 for light dining

1 cup sour cream
4 T butter
3 garlic, pressed
20 threads saffron (.2 g)
2 t chicken stock base
1 t habanero pepper (jar), seeded and minced
¼ lb. angel hair
2 eggs
4 eggbeaters
½ cup Kalamata olives, pitted and chopped
1 cup arugula leaves, chopped
1 cup soft Italian Fontina, grated
½ cup Parmesan, grated
2 T butter for pan

Drain sour cream in strainer overnight.
Melt butter and heat garlic on low for 1 minute.
Mix in saffron, stock base, and habanero. Keep warm.
Cook angel hair in boiling water.
Rinse in hot water, drain, then add to saffron butter. Let sit 5 minutes.
Mix all eggs with warm pasta.
Add olives, arugula, and both cheeses.
Heat 10" non-stick skillet on medium then butter lightly. Spread pasta mixture evenly.
Cook on medium-low, centering flame under each quarter for 4 minutes – 16 minutes this side.
Off heat, place slightly larger platter over skillet and flip. Push and slide frittata back onto re-buttered pan. Again, move heat around edges and cook 10 minutes total this side.
Slide off, cool, then chill overnight.
Discard irregular edges, and cut into small wedges. Place on greased pan.
Proceed, Refrigerate, or Freeze.

1 red onion, cut in small wedges
1 T lime juice
½ t sugar
½ t salt

Mix onion, lime, sugar, and salt in baggie.
Seal, removing air, and marinate for 1 hour.

Bake at 350 for 5 minutes.
Pipe or spoon sour cream onto wedges.
Top with onion.

Crispy Critters

Lamb Racks in a Rosemary Crust with a Dijon Glaze

Spiced Beef Wellingtons

Peking Duck and Scallions in Couscous Cups

Yukon Gold Ginger Cakes with Sour Cream and Caviar or Hoisin Sauce

Crispy Buttermilk Pecan Chicken with a Curried Horseradish Dip

Sherried Lobster Newburg with Leeks in Vol-au-Vent Shells

Spicy Stuffed Mushrooms with Tomatillos

Spanish Clams Casino in Black Rye Cups

Moroccan Swordfish

Tonkatsu with a Tamarind Dip

Lamb Racks in a Rosemary Crust with Dijon
makes 22 chops or serves 6 for light dining

3 racks of lamb, frenched

Slice lamb between bones (7 or 8 chops each rack) and flatten to ½" with smooth mallet. Lay in 2 zip baggies.

1 T chicken stock base
1/3 cup hot water
2 T cornstarch
1/3 cup cold water
4 garlic, pressed
1 t black pepper
¼ t thyme, ground
¼ cup vegetable oil

Mix stock base with hot water. Mix cornstarch with cold water. Combine.
Add garlic, pepper, thyme, and oil.
Divide mixture evenly between baggies.
Zip removing air and chill overnight (lay flat).
Turn a couple times to mix cornstarch (before bedtime and in morning).

1 cup flour
5 eggs
¼ t salt
3 cups panko bread crumbs
1 T fresh rosemary, minced
1 t black pepper

Put flour in bowl.
Beat eggs with salt.

Mix panko with rosemary and pepper.
Pull out chop, dredge in flour (tap off), dip in egg, then press in panko.
Lay out in single layer and chill ½ hour.

1 cup vegetable oil

Heat oil and cook on medium-high for 1 minute each side.
Proceed, Refrigerate, or Freeze.

1 cup Dijon
2 T virgin olive oil

Stir oil into Dijon.
Place dollop on each chop.
Broil for 5 minutes on middle rack of oven.

Garni: deep mustard color bean threads, grape tomatoes
Note: You might want cocktail plates with these.

Spiced Beef Wellingtons on Red Bean Threads

Spiced Beef Wellingtons

(adapted from the recipe of Alexandra Haagensen)
makes 36 pieces or serves 2 for light dining

1 t paprika	Combine paprika, pepper, chili, and cumin.
1 t black pepper	Season beef evenly.
1 t dark chili powder	Chill overnight.
1 t cumin	
1 lb. beef tenderloin, well-trimmed and cut into ¾" pieces	
1 T lime juice	Zap lime juice for 10 seconds.
20 saffron threads (.2 g)	Crumble saffron into lime.
6 oz. cream cheese, soft	Let sit for 15 minutes.
1 shallot minced	Combine cream cheese, saffron in lime, shallot, and salt. Chill to firm.
¼ t salt	
2 sheets Pepperidge Farm frozen puff pastry sheets (thawed in fridge overnight) or shells for light dining	Roll out one pastry sheet on a floured surface to 10 x 12. Poke all over with fork. Brush with water and fold in half.
½ cup flour for dusting	Press together lightly with rolling pin. Poke all over again with fork. Make 1 ½" cut-outs. Place on pan.
1 egg	Mix egg and cream. Brush on pastry.
2 T heavy cream	Sprinkle with pepper.
black pepper	Bake at 425 for 11 minutes. If some topple over, realign, and cool. Repeat with other pastry sheet. Poke finger in center to make cup.
2 T vegetable oil	Toss beef in oil then salt evenly.
½ t salt	Broil for 3 minutes. Pipe saffron cream into shells and place on greased pan. Top with warm beef.
	Bake at 325 for 3 minutes.

Peking Duck with Scallions in Couscous Cups

(adapted from Incredible Cuisine – Jean-Pierre Brehier)
makes 36 pieces or serves 2 for light dining

1 whole duck breast, boneless and skinless 1 T vegetable oil ½ t salt ½ t onion powder ½ t garlic powder ½ t black pepper	Roll duck in oil. Season both sides with salt, onion, garlic, and pepper. Cover with wax paper. Bake at 375 for 30 minutes. Chill in juices. Cut into thin strips. Toss in juices.
2 cups chicken stock (1 t base per 1 cup water) 1 garlic, pressed 10 oz. couscous	Boil liquid stock. Add garlic and couscous then cover. Let sit off heat for 5 minutes.
4 eggs ¼ cup Parmesan, grated 1 t black pepper	Mix eggs with Parmesan and pepper. Add couscous. Fill and press into greased mini-muffin pans. Bake at 350 for 10 minutes. Cool. Transfer to greased pan.
½ cup hoisin sauce (Koon Chun) 1 T sherry 8 scallions, minced	Mix hoisin with sherry. Mix duck with scallions. Spoon hoisin onto couscous cups. Top with duck strips. Proceed, Refrigerate, or Freeze. Bake at 300 for 5 minutes.

Garni: pickled ginger or a bowl of edamame beans.
Options: You'll only need less than half the couscous for light dining.
Press it into 2 larger containers and cook for 15 minutes.

Yukon Gold Ginger Cakes with Sour Cream and Caviar

makes 48 pieces

4" fresh ginger, peeled

3 eggs

1/3 cup vegetable oil

1 sweet onion, grated and squeezed dry

1/3 cup matzo meal

1 t baking powder

2 t black pepper

1 ½ t salt

Pulse ginger 'til minced.

In bowl, mix ginger with eggs, oil, onion pulp, matzo, baking powder, pepper, and salt.

2 lbs. Yukon Gold potatoes, peeled and cut

Pulse potatoes to a fine chop.

Stir into egg mixture.

Fill greased mini-muffin cups.

Press plastic wrap on remaining batter to prevent discoloring if cooking in batches.

Bake at 400 for 30 minutes, switching upper and lower racks midway.

Proceed, Refrigerate, or Freeze.

1 c sour cream

4 oz. salmon roe and sevruga caviar

(or 8 oz. hoisin sauce)

chopped chives

Heat at 350 for 5 minutes.

Top with 1 teaspoon sour cream and ½ teaspoon of caviar.

(or with hoisin alone).

Sprinkle with chives.

Garni: sugar snap peas, asparagus, or pickled ginger

Options: Bake in full-sized muffin cups for light dining and cook for 40 minutes.

Crispy Buttermilk Pecan Chicken with a Curried Horseradish Dip
makes 36 pieces or serves 5 for light dining

2 lbs. chicken thighs, boneless and skinless	Cut chicken into 1" strips.
	Cover with buttermilk.
1 cup buttermilk	Chill overnight.
1 cup pecans	Bake pecan at 350 for 10 minutes. Cool and finely chop.
1 ½ cups flour	Combine flour with adobo, pepper, cumin, and onion powder.
1 ½ T adobo seasoning	
1 T black pepper	Drain chicken and toss in flour.
1 T cumin	Remove and shake off excess flour.
1 T onion powder	Lay out in single layer.
½ cup vegetable oil	Heat oil and cook chicken on medium-high for 1 ½ minutes each side.
	Drain on paper towel.
	Sprinkle with pecans.
	Proceed, Refrigerate, or Freeze.
	Bake at 450 for 4 minutes.

Curried Horseradish Dip

½ cup Hickory Farms horseradish sauce	Mix all ingredients.
1 T Madras curry powder	Chill overnight for curry to blend.
2 T well-drained horseradish	
¼ t sugar	
1/8 t salt	

Options: Omit curry for a beef sauce. Omit pecans for a simpler 'fried' chicken.
Note: Don't cut chicken too small or flour dredge will overwhelm it.
Halve chicken thighs only and cook for 3 minutes each side for light dining.

Crispy Buttermilk Chicken with a Thai Peanut Dip

Sherried Lobster Newburg with Leeks in Vol-au-vent Shells

(adapted from Locke-Ober's Café – Ned and Pam Bradford)
makes 36 pieces or serves 2 for light dining

2 T butter	Melt 2 T butter then cook flour on low for 5 minutes. Add tomato paste, stock base, then add milk slowly.
1 T flour	
½ t tomato paste	
1 ½ t fish stock base	
¾ cup milk	Cook on low 5 minutes.
2 T butter	Melt 2 T butter and cook leeks on medium-low for 5 minutes.
1 leek, white only, minced	
½ t paprika	Add paprika, cayenne, sherry, and cognac.
¼ t cayenne	Heat on medium for 5 minutes. Add cream and heat 'til reduced by ¼.
¼ cup sherry	
1 T excellent cognac	
½ cup heavy cream	Combine sauces, cool, and chill.
1 lb. fresh lobster meat, preferably knuckle or tail	Chop lobster (not for light dining). Moisten with enough sauce to bind.
2 sheets Pepperidge Farm frozen puff pastry sheets (thawed in fridge overnight) or use shells for light dining	Roll out one pastry sheet on a floured surface to 10 x 12. Poke all over with fork. Brush with water and fold in half.
½ cup flour for dusting	Press together lightly with rolling pin. Poke all over again with fork. Make 1 ½" cut-outs. Place on pan. Mix egg and cream. Brush on pastry.
1 egg	
2 T heavy cream	
	Bake at 425 for 11 minutes. If some topple over, realign, and cool. Repeat with other pastry sheet. Poke finger in center to make cup. Place on greased pan. Fill with lobster.
4 parsley sprigs	Top with parsley. Bake at 325 for 4 minutes.

Options: Make 3" cut-outs for light dining and leave knuckles whole.

Spicy Stuffed Mushrooms with Tomatillos
(adapted from The Boston Globe - Phil Grenadier)
makes 25 pieces or serves 2 for light dining

4 slices smoked bacon	Cook bacon 'til crisp. Drain on paper towel and reserve.
1 jalapeno, cut up with seeds 1 red pepper, cut up ½ t habanero (jar), no seeds and minced 1 garlic, pressed 3 tomatillos, washed and cut up	Pulse jalapeno, red pepper, habanero, garlic, and tomatillos to fine chop. Reserve.
4 oz. provolone	Process provolone to fine chop. Add to peppers.
2 T lime juice 1 t chicken stock base ¼ cup panko bread crumbs ¼ cup fresh cilantro, chopped	Zap lime 20 seconds and add stock base. Add to peppers with panko and cilantro. Chop bacon and add.
25 white button mushrooms (1" width)	Remove stem and widen opening in mushrooms with melon ball utensil or knife. Stuff mushrooms and place on foil-lined pan. Bake at 450 for 10 minutes. Place on double paper towels. Cool. Place on fresh paper towels. Chill. Proceed, Refrigerate, or Freeze. Bake at 350 for 5 minutes.

Garni: peeled and sliced portabellas, grape tomatoes
Options: Fill halved poblano peppers instead for light dining. Drizzle with olive oil and bake for 35 minutes. Remove jalapeno seeds for a calmer version. Omit bacon for meatless option.

Spanish Clams Casino in Black Rye Cups
makes 36 pieces or serves 3 for light dining

2 T white wine	Zap wine for 20 seconds.
40 threads saffron (.4 g)	Crumble saffron into wine.
	Zap another 10 seconds.
	Let sit 15 minutes.
6 slices smoked bacon	Cook bacon 'til crisp and remove.
4 T butter	Discard all but 2 T fat.
2 shallots, minced	Add butter and cook shallots on medium-low for 5 minutes.
2 garlic, pressed	
¼ t black pepper	Add garlic, pepper, cayenne, fish base, and lemon zest.
¼ t cayenne	
1 ½ t fish stock base	Warm on low for 1 minute.
1 lemon zest, minced	Crumble bacon. Add with saffron wine, chilies, egg, egg yolk, and clams.
2 T green chilies (jar), chopped	
1 egg	
1 egg yolk	
1 lb. fresh clams, drained and chopped	
2 cups panko bread crumbs	Fold in panko and sage.
1 T fresh sage, minced	Toss to combine. Cool.
1 cup shredded cheddar (orange)	Fold in cheese. Chill.
1 loaf Pepperidge Farm pumpernickel	Make 2" bread cut-outs and roll flat. Press into greased mini-muffin pans.
	Bake at 350 for 8 minutes. Cool.
	Fill cups with clams.
	Proceed, Refrigerate, or Freeze.
	Bake at 450 for 5 minutes.

Note: Canned clams may be used, but if they're salty decrease stock base slightly.
Options: Fill individual flan dishes or shells for light dining and cook for 15 minutes.
The bread cup isn't necessary.

Spanish Clams Casino

Moroccan Swordfish
makes 35 pieces or serves 2 for light dining

½ cup buttermilk
2 T lime juice
1 lb. swordfish, cut into 1" cubes

Mix buttermilk and lime. Add swordfish and chill for ½ hour.

Spice Mix:
2 T salt
1 T paprika
1 t white pepper
2 t onion powder
2 t garlic powder
1 t cayenne
1 t thyme, ground

Combine salt, paprika, pepper, onion, garlic, cayenne, and thyme.

1 T curry powder
1/8 t cardamom
1/3 cup flour

Mix ¼ cup spice mix with curry, cardamom, and flour.
Drain swordfish and toss in spiced flour mix, pressing it on.
Lay out in single layer.

¼ cup vegetable oil

Heat oil and cook swordfish on medium for 1 minute each of 2 sides.
Drain on paper towel.
Proceed, Refrigerate, or Freeze.

Saffron Lime Sauce

Bake at 350 for 5 minutes.
Serve with Saffron Lime Sauce
(see Spicy Pork Sausage)

Garni: broccoli and Colby cheese strips
Note: Don't use toothpicks with these.

Moroccan Swordfish with a Saffron Lime Dip

*Tonkatsu with a Tamarind Dip and
Yukon Gold Ginger Cakes with Sour Cream or Hoisin*

Tonkatsu (Japanese Pork Strips) with a Tamarind Sauce

makes 24 pieces or serves 2 for light dining

4 thinly sliced pork chops, boneless	Lay out pork and pound both sides with dimpled side of tenderizing mallet.
3 garlic, pressed	Rub garlic over pork with fork. Scrape off and discard.

¼ cup flour	Mix flour with salt and pepper.
¼ t salt	
¼ t black pepper	
2 eggs	Beat eggs with salt.
¼ t salt	
1 cup panko bread crumbs	Mix panko with pepper and parsley.
½ t black pepper	Dredge pork in flour then shake-off.
1 T fresh flat parsley, chopped	Dunk in eggs and lift out.
	Coat with panko, pressing on.
	Lay out flat then chill ½ hour.

½ cup vegetable oil	Heat oil and cook pork on medium-high for 1 minute each side.
	Proceed, Refrigerate, or Freeze.
	Bake at 450 for 5 minutes.
	Cut in strips and serve with sauce.

Tamarind Sauce

1 cup Heinz ketchup	Combine ketchup, pepper.
½ t black pepper	Worcestershire, and lemon.
2 T Worcestershire sauce	Chill ½ hour.
1 t lemon juice	

Cold Canapés

Lemon, Garlic, and Dill Shrimp Cocktail with a Spicy Cocktail Sauce

Sherried Shallot Liver Pureé on Red Apples

Scallop Citrus Ceviche in Belgian Endive

Spicy Steak Tartare

Smoked Salmon Mousse on Cukes with Horseradish Cream

Lemon Coconut Rice Slices with Tuna Tartare

Rolled Saffron Crepes with Jalapenos

Prosciutto and Shaved Parmesan with Tomato and Basil Leaf

Lemon, Garlic, and Dill Shrimp Cocktail with a Spicy Cocktail Sauce

(adapted from the recipe of Ann Lawson)
makes 42 pieces

2 T balsamic vinegar (Monari or other non-aged)
2 T lemon juice
1 garlic, pressed
½ t black pepper
1 pack Good Seasons Italian Salad Dressing mix
2 T oil

Mix vinegar, lemon, garlic, pepper, and Good Seasons mix.
Shake well and add oil.
Let sit 1 hour...better yet overnight.

2 lbs. large shrimp, cooked and tail off
¼ cup fresh dill, chopped

Toss shrimp in marinade with dill.
Baggie tightly and chill 'til ready to use (best within 2 hours).
Pour off liquid before serving with cocktail dipping sauce.

Note: Aged vinegar is too strong and makes the shrimp very dark

Spicy Cocktail Sauce

1 cup Heinz ketchup
1 T red wine vinegar
3 T horseradish, drained
½ t red chili powder
½ t cayenne

Mix ketchup, vinegar, horseradish, chili powder, and cayenne.
Chill 1 hour.

Garni: a bed of green leaf lettuce, grape tomatoes

Sherried Liver Pureé on Red Apples

Sherried Shallot Liver Pureé on Red Apples

makes 50 pieces

1 envelope Knox gelatin	Sprinkle gelatin over Marsala.
¼ cup dry Marsala wine	Let soften 5 minutes.
	Cook in boiling water bath for 5 minutes 'til clear. Cool slightly.
3 T butter	Melt butter and cook shallots on medium-low for 5 minutes.
2 shallots, minced	
1 lb. chicken livers, rinsed and drained	Add liver, garlic, bay leaf, and thyme. Cook on medium-low for 12 minutes.
1 garlic, pressed	
¼ t bay leaf, ground	
¼ t thyme, ground	
¼ cup excellent cognac	Lift out livers then add cognac to pan. Reduce on med-high 'til very moist.
2 t chicken stock base	
½ t black pepper	Add stock base, pepper, then cool.
½ cup cottage cheese	
2 T fresh flat parsley, minced	Process cottage cheese 'til smooth.
	Re-drain livers and process with cheese, cognac, then gelatin 'til smooth.
1 cup merlot red wine	Add parsley and chill overnight.
1 T lemon juice	Heat wine with lemon, sugar, nutmeg, cinnamon, and cloves to boiling. Cool.
3 T sugar	
½ t nutmeg	
½ t cinnamon	Slice red apples and toss in wine.
¼ t cloves	Chill in tightly sealed baggie 'til needed.
2 red delicious apples	
	Pipe liver onto drained apples.

Garni: wedges of sharp cheddar, green grapes
Options: This makes a more authentic substitute for the saffron cream in Spiced Beef Wellingtons. Try it for light dining only, as it will be less popular with a crowd.

Scallop Citrus Ceviche in Belgian Endive

makes 30 pieces or serves 4 for light dining

¼ red and yellow pepper, minced	Squeeze peppers dry in paper towel.
1 lb. sea scallops	Remove muscle if attached to side of scallop, rinse, drain, then chop evenly.
½ cup lime juice 1 T white vinegar 1 jalapeno, mostly seeded and minced ¼ red onion, minced	Mix lime, vinegar, jalapeno, onion, sweet peppers, and scallops. Chill for 4 hours with plastic wrap pressed on surface.
½ orange zest, minced 1 orange, segments only, chopped and drained ¼ cup fresh cilantro, chopped 2 t sugar ½ t salt ¼ t black pepper	Pour off most of juice. Add orange zest, segments, cilantro, sugar, salt, and pepper. Chill ½ hour.
4 heads Belgian endive	Trim ends from endive and lay out 'petals' in concentric circles on a platter. Lift ceviche from liquid and fill endive.

Garni: cubes of feta and orange bean threads
Options: Serve on petals of Bibb lettuce in Lemon Vinaigrette (see Grilled Salmon Salad) for light dining.

Scallop Ceviche in Belgian Endive

Spicy Steak Tartare

Spicy Steak Tartare
makes 24 pieces or serves 2 for light dining

1 T light olive oil
2 t red wine vinegar
1 t lemon juice
1 t Dijon
¼ t Tabasco
2 T ketchup
1 T Worcestershire Sauce
½ t salt
½ t black pepper

Mix liquids and sauces with salt and pepper.
Chill for 4 hours.

1 T scallions (4)
1 T capers
1 T cornichons (4)
6 sprigs parsley

Mince scallions, capers, cornichons, and 4 sprigs only of parsley.

Proceed or Refrigerate.

½ lb. sirloin, ground the day of use
4 slices country white bread

Mix all ingredients above with beef.
Cut 1" bread rounds.

2 T butter for pan

Heat butter in skillet and cook bread on medium for 1 minute each side. Cool.
Mound beef onto bread.
Top with parsley leaf.

Garni: cornichons, grape tomatoes, sliced red onion on pale blue bean threads
Note: Select your own steak and have the market trim and grind it, guaranteeing the cut of beef and its freshness.
Options: Place mound of beef on baby arugula in Lemon Vinaigrette (see Grilled Salmon Salad) for light dining. Serve with larger toast points.

Smoked Salmon Mousse on Cukes with Horseradish Cream

makes 40 pieces

2 seedless cukes, partially peeled

Slice cukes on diagonal and lay on double paper towel.
Top with paper towel and cover.
Chill overnight.

1 lb. smoked salmon
8 T butter, very soft
2 T lemon juice
¼ t cayenne
¼ t black pepper
½ sweet onion, grated and squeezed
¼ cup heavy cream

Process salmon to mince then remove.
Process butter, lemon, cayenne, and pepper.
Add salmon, onion, and cream.
Pulse to combine.

1 T fresh dill, chopped

Stir in dill.
Lay out 2 sheets of plastic wrap on counter (14" long).
Form a 1" log across middle of each and wrap tightly, folding in ends to seal.
Chill overnight.
Proceed, Refrigerate, or Freeze.

2 T horseradish, well-strained
2 T Hickory Farms horseradish sauce
3 sprigs flat parsley

Mix horseradish and sauce.
Slice salmon and place on cukes.
Top with horseradish and parsley.

Garni: snow peas and orange peppers with orange bean threads
Note: Don't assemble these in advance...cukes get soggy.

Smoked Salmon Mousse on Cukes

Lemon Coconut Rice Slices with Cilantro and Lobster Knuckles

Lemon Coconut Rice Slices with Tuna Tartare
(adapted from James McNair's Rice Cookbook)
makes 36 pieces

14 oz. unsweetened coconut milk	Combine coconut milk and water.
8 oz. water	Boil and add well-rinsed rice.
1 cup arborio rice	Cover and cook on low for 25 minutes, undisturbed.
¼ t Boyajian lemon oil	Add lemon oil, salt and pepper.
¾ t salt	Cool 15 minutes.
½ t black pepper	
3 -12" lengths aluminum foil	Lay out foil and spoon 8" x 1 ½" rice logs across center of each sheet.
	Form evenly with cold, wet fingers.
	Roll up, folding in edges.
	Steam for 1 hour.
	Chill overnight.

Tuna Tartare

2 T rice vinegar	Mix vinegar, ketchup, Worcestershire, and black pepper.
2 T ketchup	
1 T Worcestershire	
1 t black pepper	
2 T red onion, finely chopped	Mix onion, jalapenos, and tuna with sauce.
2 jalapenos, no seeds, finely chopped	Chill 4 hours.
½ lb. sushi grade tuna, chopped	Add cilantro.
1 T fresh cilantro, finely chopped	Slice rice into ½" rounds and top with tuna and tomato.
5 grape tomatoes, cut into 8 strips each	

Options: Top rice slice with cilantro cream (see Sweet Potato Fritters) and lobster knuckles. Tuna tartare is also great served in Belgian endive for light dining.

Rolled Saffron Crepes with Jalapenos
makes 50 pieces

¼ cup water
40 saffron threads (.4 g)

Zap water for 20 seconds.
Crumble saffron into it.
Zap another 10 seconds.
Let sit 15 minutes.
Beat eggs. Add saffron, butter, and pepper.
Mix in flour and salt, beating.
Stir in milk 'til smooth. Let sit ½ hour.

2 eggs
2 T butter, melted
1 T black pepper
½ cup flour
¼ t salt
3/4 cup milk
2 T butter for pan

Heat a 12" skillet to hot then butter.
Pour an even, thin layer of batter over bottom surface. Cook 1 minute and flip.
Cook 1 minute more then remove. Repeat making 5 crepes.
Do not stack crepes 'til cool.

1 envelope Knox gelatin
¼ cup lemon juice

Sprinkle gelatin over lemon juice.
Let sit 5 minutes. Cook in boiling water bath for 5 minutes 'til clear.
Cool 20 minutes, stirring occasionally.

½ orange, yellow, and red pepper, minced and squeezed dry in paper towels
16 oz. cream cheese, soft
1 grated onion with juice
2 jalapenos, no seeds, minced
½ t salt
¼ cup fresh cilantro, minced

Add peppers to cream cheese with onion, jalapenos, salt, and cilantro.
Mix in gelatin and chill to a very thick batter consistency, about ½ hour, stirring occasionally.
Spread filling over entire crepe and roll up.
Repeat.
Wrap and chill overnight.
Slice into 1" diagonal pieces. Lie flat.

Options: Top a few with Salmon Caviar.

Rolled Saffron Crepes

Prosciutto and Shaved Parmesan with Tomato and Basil Leaf

makes 32 pieces

4 oz. cream cheese, soft
2 t lemon juice
½ sweet onion, grated and squeezed dry
½ t black pepper
pinch salt

Mix cream cheese with lemon, onion, pepper, and salt.
Chill to firm.

8 slices country white bread
16 paper-thin slices imported prosciutto
½ lb. Parmesan, thinly shaved in 1" pieces

Cut-out 32 - 1 ½" rounds from bread.
Pipe or spread on cheese.
Drape ½ prosciutto slice on cheese.
Place Parmesan piece on top.

10 grape tomatoes, thinly sliced
1 bunch fresh basil leaves

Top with a small dollop of cream cheese, then tomato, then small basil leaf.
Lay out on and top with moistened paper towels.

Cover with plastic wrap.
Chill 4 hours.

Note: These improve and firm up after 4 hours.
Bring to room temp before serving.
Options: Make some without prosciutto for vegetarians.
These are delicious briefly broiled, but place the parmesan atop the tomato and basil.

Finger Sandwiches

Spicy Goat Cheese and Prosciutto Croque Monsieurs

Lobster Knuckles with Lime and Shallots in Hot Dog Rolls

Crab and Shrimp Salad with Lemon, Ranch Dressing

Onion and Garlic Roasted Tenderloin with Béarnaise Mayo on Sourdough Bread

Roast Turkey and Lemon Thyme Stuffing with Cranberry Sauce

Grilled Salmon Salad Pitas with Capers and Peppercorn Pyrennes Cheese

Hummus, Spinach, and Roasted Pepper Pitas

Croque Monsieurs with Prosciutto Canapés, Parmesan Canapés, and Sun-ripened Tomatoes

Spicy Goat Cheese and Prosciutto Croque Monsieurs

makes 40 pieces or serves 4 for light dining

3 ripe tomatoes	Halve tomatoes, squeeze out seeds, remove stem, chop, then salt.
¼ t salt	Let sit in strainer for 15 minutes.
8 oz. cream cheese soft	Combine cheeses with black pepper, cayenne, rosemary, and parsley.
3 oz. goat cheese, soft	Tap all moisture from tomatoes.
1 t black pepper	Add to cheese.
¼ t cayenne	
1 t fresh rosemary, minced	
1 T fresh flat parsley, chopped	
10 slices paper-thin imported prosciutto	Chop prosciutto and add to cheese.
10 slices white country bread	Lay out 5 slices of bread.
	Spread cheese on bread.
	Top with another slice.
6 T butter for pan	Heat skillet to medium and butter.
	Cook sandwiches for 1-2 minutes.
	Lift, re-butter pan, and flip.
	Cook 1-2 minutes more. Chill.
	Trim crust and cut into 8 wedges.
	Proceed, Refrigerate, or Freeze.
	Bake at 350 for 4 minutes.

Garni: grape tomatoes and fresh rosemary sprig
Options: Eliminate prosciutto for vegetarian croques.
Trim crusts and quarter sandwiches for light dining.

Lobster Knuckles with Shallots in Hot Dog Rolls
makes 16 pieces or serves 2 for light dining

¼ cup Hellman's mayo
2 t lime juice
2 t Hidden Valley Ranch Mix
1 T shallot, minced
¼ t paprika
2 T celery leaf, pale green only, minced
2 T sour cream
2 T fresh chives, minced
1 lb. fresh lobster meat (preferably knuckles), coarsely chopped
4 hot dog rolls, flat-sided

Stir mayo then add lime.

Add ranch mix, shallot, paprika, celery leaf, sour cream, and 1 T chives.
Chill 4 hours.
Moisten lobster with mayo to bind.
Chill for 4 hours.
Fill hot dog rolls and stand in pan lined with moistened paper towels. Top with moistened paper towels. Chill 4 hours. Cut each into 4 pieces. Stand on platter.
Sprinkle with chives.

Crab and Shrimp Salad with Lemon Dressing
makes 24 pieces or serves 4 for light dining

½ cup Hellman's mayonnaise
2 T lemon juice
2 T Hidden Valley Ranch Mix
½ sweet onion, grated and squeezed dry
¼ t paprika
1/8 t cayenne
3 T sour cream
2 T fresh dill, coarsely chopped
1 lb. medium cooked shrimp, tail off
½ lb. fresh all leg crab meat (picked over and squeezed of excess moisture)
1 loaf Pepperidge Farm thin sliced white bread

Stir mayo. Add lemon, ranch mix, onion, paprika, cayenne, sour cream, then dill.

Pulse shrimp to coarse chop.
Stir in crab and mayo mix.
Chill overnight.
Remove crust from bread.
Make sandwiches then wrap in moist paper towels.
Cover and chill for at least 4 hours.
Slice diagonally into quarters.
Serve cold.

Roast Tenderloin with Béarnaise on Sourdough

makes 30 pieces or serves 6 for light dining

4 lb. beef tenderloin roast, untied	Trim beef of all fat and blue skin.
2 T vegetable oil	Trim for uniform width. Roll in oil.
2 t salt	Season with salt, garlic, onion, then pepper on both sides. Let sit for 30 minutes.
2 t garlic powder	
2 t onion powder	Bake beef at 450 for 30 minutes.
2 t black pepper	For light dining, let sit 10 minutes before carving. For sandwiches, chill overnight before carving.
1 cup Hellman's mayonnaise	Stir mayo. Add lemon, shallot reduction, salt, pepper, and food coloring.
1 T lemon juice	
2 T shallot reduction (see Beef Tenderloin with Béarnaise Sauce)	Chill overnight.
¼ t salt	Cut beef into ½" slices, cutting larger ones in half. Toss in pan juices.
¼ t black pepper	Cut sourdough into ¼" slices. Lay out on counter. Top each slice with 1 t mayo.
2 drops yellow food coloring	
2 baguettes of sourdough bread	Place beef on half of the bread.
	Top with other half. Wrap in moist paper towels. Cover and chill for 4 hours.

Options: Serve Sliced Tenderloin with Horseradish Sauce (no curry) and Béarnaise Sauce for light dining.

Cranberry Sauce for Turkey

(adapted from the recipe of Ruth Nelson)

4 cups cleaned cranberries	Boil cranberries in water and lemon for 20 minutes.
1 ½ cups water	
2 T lemon juice	Strain through food mill.
1 cup sugar	Add sugar, brown sugar, and maple.
1 cup brown sugar	Cook on medium for 10 minutes.
1 t maple flavoring	Chill overnight.

Roast Turkey and Stuffing with Cranberry Sauce
makes 24 pieces or serves 4 for light dining

4 cups cold water
1 T salt
2 t sugar
6 lb. turkey breast, boneless and split
1 T vegetable oil
1 t garlic powder
2 t onion powder
1 t paprika
1 t adobo seasoning
1 t black pepper
4 T butter
3 stalks celery, strings peeled off and finely chopped
1 sweet onion, finely chopped
2 T fresh sage, minced
2 t fresh rosemary, minced
2 t fresh lemon thyme, minced
1 t black pepper
1 cup chicken stock
(1 t base per 1 cup water)
¼ cup white wine
1 egg
16 oz. Pepperidge Farm herb stuffing

Mix salt and sugar in water 'til dissolved.
Immerse turkey breasts. Chill overnight.
Roll dry turkey in oil.
Season underside with garlic, onion, and paprika.
Season skin side with adobo and pepper.
Let sit for 30 minutes.
Cover with wax paper. Bake at 325 for 40 minutes. Roll in juices and cook for 20 minutes.
Uncover and reserve pan juices. Chill overnight.
Melt butter and cook celery and onion on medium for 10 minutes. Add sage, rosemary, lemon thyme, pepper, liquid stock, wine, and egg.
Pour over stuffing and toss briefly.
Sprinkle with turkey juices 'til very moist. Chill overnight.

To assemble:
2 cups Hellman's mayo
1 T lemon juice
½ t black pepper
12 whole wheat rolls, sliced top to bottom, ends discarded
(each roll yields 4 slices)

Slice turkey breasts into ¼" slices.
Cut to fit bread rounds.
Mix mayo, lemon, and pepper.
Lay out 24 bread slices and spread with mayo.
Place turkey on mayo. Top with cranberry sauce (previous page). Top with stuffing.
Top with bread spread with mayo.
Wrap sandwiches in moist paper towel, then cover with plastic. Chill 1 hour.

Grilled Salmon Salad with Peppercorn Cheese
makes 10 pieces or serves 2 for light dining

1 lb. salmon filet
1 T vegetable oil
¾ t adobo seasoning
¼ t black pepper
¼ cup Hellmann's mayo
2 T lime
1 T Hidden Valley Ranch Mix
¼ t paprika
1/8 t cayenne
½ sweet onion, grated and squeezed dry
¼ cup sour cream
1 T fresh dill, chopped
2 T small capers
10 arugula leaves, cut in ribbons
¼ cup lemon vinaigrette
5 mini-pitas, halved
1 lb. peppercorn Pyrennes cheese, thinly sliced

Roll salmon in oil and season with adobo and pepper.
Grill over medium coals for 4 minutes each side. Chill. Flake.
Stir mayo. Add lime and ranch mix.
Add paprika, cayenne, onion pulp, sour cream, and dill. Chill.

Toss salmon with enough dressing to moisten. Add capers.
Toss arugula in vinaigrette.
Lay a cheese strip against one side of pita then fill salmon salad against it.
Press some arugula in top.
Stand in pan lined with moist paper towels.
Top with moist paper towels. Wrap and chill for 4 hours.

Lemon Vinaigrette

3 shallots
2 T Dijon
1 cup red wine vinegar
½ cup lemon juice
½ t sugar
2 t salt
1 cup vegetable oil
½ cup olive oil

Process shallots to mince.
Add Dijon, vinegar, lemon, sugar, and salt.

With motor running, slowly add oils to emulsify.

Hummus, Spinach, and Roasted Pepper Pitas

makes 10 pieces or serves 3 for light dining

15 oz. chick peas (can), drained, reserve liquid
2 T lemon juice
½ t white vinegar
1 T tahini or sesame paste
1 garlic, pressed
1/8 t cayenne
¼ t salt

Process peas, lemon, vinegar, and enough reserved liquid (3 T) to thick pureé.
Add tahini, garlic, cayenne, and salt.
Process 2 minutes. Chill overnight.

Roasted Red Peppers

2 red peppers, seeded and halved
3 T virgin olive oil
3 garlic, smashed intact
½ t salt

To assemble:
1 bunch fresh spinach
10 mini-pitas

Press peppers flat on pan, skin up. Broil 'til black. Cool. Wipe off skin (rinse hands but keep peppers dry). Cut into thin strips.
Mix oil, garlic, and salt. Add peppers.
Chill overnight. Discard garlic
Cut spinach into ribbons then clean.
Toss in Lemon Vinaigrette (see Grilled Salmon Salad).
Half fill pitas with hummus.
Top with peppers, lifted from oil.
Top with spinach.
Stand in pan lined with moist paper towels.
Top with moist paper towels. Wrap and chill for 4 hours.

Note: I use Goya canned chick peas. 'All natural' brands often lack the sodium, which you'll only have to add in the end.

Sweets

Chocolate Chip Oatmeal Cookies with Almonds and Coconut

Viennese Lemon Cakes

White Chocolate Bark with Cranberries and Pistachios

Tuaca-Laced Gingerbread with Lemon Cream

Walnut Carrot Cake with Cream Cheese Frosting

Baby Key Lime Pies with a Chocolate Cardamom Crust

Soft Chocolate Espresso Clouds

Pecan Brownies

Amazing Chocolate Chip Cookies

Chocolate Chip and Oatmeal Cookies

(adapted from Gourmet Magazine)
makes 32 large cookies

¾ cup sliced almonds
2 sticks butter, soft
1 cup brown sugar
½ cup sugar
2 eggs
2 t vanilla
½ t baking soda
¼ t salt
1 cup flour
2 cups old-fashioned oats
1 cup shredded coconut
2 cups semi-sweet chocolate chips
wax paper

Bake almonds at 325 for 10 minutes. Beat butter and both sugars in mixer on medium-high for 4 minutes. Add eggs. Mix on low. Add vanilla, baking soda, and salt.
Mix on low. Add flour. Mix on low.
Finely chop almonds.
Combine with oats, coconut, and chocolate chips. Stir in cookie dough.
Line pan with wax paper and drop 8 mounds of 2 T dough each.
Bake at 375 for 13-14 minutes on middle rack of oven. Repeat in batches.
Cool for 10 minutes then loosen with spatula and cool completely.

Viennese Lemon Cakes

(adapted from the original Cuisine Magazine)
makes 24 pieces

2 sticks cold butter, cut up
4 T sugar
1 T sour cream
1 T vanilla
2 cups flour

6 oz. Robertson's lemon curd
2 T confectioner's sugar

Pulse butter and sugar 'til chunky.
Add sour cream and vanilla.
Pulse 'til just moistened.
Add flour. Pulse 'til just crumbly.
Fill mini-muffin cups and press firmly.
Bake at 350 for 18 minutes. Immediately press indentation in center for curd. Cool completely.
Loosen edges with a thin knife and lift out.
Proceed or Freeze.
Pipe in lemon curd. Place confectioner's sugar in a strainer and dust top of cakes.

White Chocolate Bark with Cranberries and Pistachios
(adapted from the recipe of Penny Kolgian)

1 cup raw pistachios (shelled)
1 cup dried cranberries
1 lb. fine white chocolate, chopped

Reserve 20 of the greenest pistachios for the top. Bake remaining at 350 for 10 minutes.
Steam cranberries for 4 minutes. Blot dry.
Reserve 20 for the top.
Melt chocolate in double boiler.
Add nuts and cranberries (not reserved ones).
Stir then spread onto sheet pan in single layer.
Immediately decorate top with reserved nuts and berries, pressing slightly.
Chill uncovered for 4 hours.
Break into large bite-sized pieces. Serve cold.

Tuaca-Laced Gingerbread with Lemon Cream
makes 24 pieces

8 oz. cream cheese, soft
4 T butter, soft
1 cup powdered sugar
½ t Boyajian lemon oil
2 t baking soda
½ cup buttermilk
¼ cup vegetable oil
1 cup sugar
3 eggs
1 cup dark molasses
2 cups flour
1 T ginger, powdered
1 t cloves
½ t cinnamon
½ t salt
1 cup boiling water
½ cup tuaca liquor
1 T nutmeg for sprinkling

Beat cheese and butter in mixer for 2 minutes.
Add powdered sugar. Mix on low. Add lemon oil. Mix on low. Chill to firm.
Sprinkle baking soda over buttermilk.
Let sit for 10 minutes 'til foaming.
Beat oil, sugar, eggs, and molasses in mixer on medium-high for 5 minutes.
Combine flour, ginger, cloves, cinnamon, and salt.
Add to mixer. Mix on low.
Add buttermilk. Mix on low.
Add boiling water. Mix on medium-low for one minute.
Pour into a greased 9x13 pan.
Bake at 350 for 40 minutes.
Cool and cut into squares.
Brush with tuaca. Pipe on lemon cream.
Sprinkle with nutmeg. Chill.

White Chocolate Bark, Brownies, Tuaca Gingerbread, and Key Lime Pies

Walnut Carrot Cake and
Viennese Lemon Cakes

Walnut Carrot Cake with Cream Cheese Frosting
(adapted from the recipe of Julie Hagan)
makes 24 pieces

1 ½ cup walnuts
1 ½ cups vegetable oil
2 cups sugar
4 eggs
2 cups flour
2 t baking soda
1 t salt
2 t cinnamon
2 t nutmeg
¼ t cloves
1 T vanilla
3 cups carrots, grated (1 lb.)

Bake walnuts at 350 for 10 minutes. Cool. Save 24 pieces for garni. Chop remainder. Combine oil and sugar. Add eggs and combine. Mix flour, baking soda, salt, cinnamon, nutmeg, and cloves. Add to eggs. Add vanilla then carrots. Add nuts. Pour into a greased 9x13 pan. Bake at 325 for 45 minutes. Cool. Cut into small triangles. Chill. Pipe on Lemon Cream Frosting (see Gingerbread) Top with walnut pieces. Serve cool.

Baby Key Lime Pies with a Chocolate Crust
(adapted from Saveur Magazine)
makes 36 mini pies

20 chocolate graham crackers
½ cup sugar
1 t cardamom
2 ½ sticks butter, melted
4 egg yolks
14 oz. sweetened condensed milk
½ cup + 2 T fresh key lime juice
(bottled is OK)
1 lime zest, minced

Process crackers to crumbs with sugar and cardamom. Add warm butter. Pulse to blend evenly. Fill greased mini-muffin cups. Press bottom and sides to form cup. Bake at 350 for 12 minutes. Press bottom down lightly again. Stir yolks and zap for 7 seconds. Stir and repeat. Stir and repeat. Beat in mixer on medium-high for 6 minutes. Slowly add condensed milk, then lime juice, then zest, mixing on low. Immediately pour into muffin cups. Chill 45 minutes in pan. Gently loosen edges with a thin knife then lift out. Chill 4 hours. Serve cold.

Soft Chocolate Espresso Clouds
(adapted from The Boston Globe - Nancy White)
makes 24 medium cookies

4 T butter
2 oz. unsweetened chocolate, chopped
2 eggs
2 t instant espresso
1 cup superfine sugar
2 t vanilla
1 cup flour
1 t baking powder
1 t cocoa powder
wax paper
1 cup confectioner's sugar

Melt butter to boiling. Off heat add chocolate. Stir to soften. Let sit to melt completely. Combine eggs, espresso, sugar, and vanilla. Beat to combine. Add chocolate. Mix flour, baking powder, and cocoa. Add to chocolate and combine. Press plastic on surface to cover. Chill overnight. Line pan with wax paper. Make 1 T cookie balls with your hands and roll in confectioner's sugar. Place cookies on pan. Bake at 350 for 12 minutes. Cool on pan.

Pecan Brownies
(adapted from Book of Great Chocolate Desserts - Maida Heatter)
makes 40 pieces

2 cups pecans
2 sticks butter
8 oz. unsweetened chocolate
5 eggs
1 T vanilla
1 T instant espresso powder
3 ½ cups sugar
1 ¾ cups flour

Bake pecans at 350 for 10 minutes. Cool and chop. Melt butter to boiling. Off heat add chocolate. Stir to soften. Let sit to melt completely. Beat eggs, vanilla, espresso powder, and sugar in mixer on medium-high for 5 minutes. Add chocolate. Mix on low. Add flour.
Mix on low. Stir in pecans.
Spread in a greased 9x13 pan.
Bake at 425 for 38 minutes on middle rack of oven. Cool completely.
Discard dark edges and cut into squares.